SPITFIRE AT WAR 3

SPITFIRE AT WAR 3

Dr ALFRED PRICE

LONDON
IAN ALLAN LTD

Contents

First published 1990

ISBN 0 7110 1933 9

Published by Ian Allan Ltd, Shepperton, Surrey;
and printed by Ian Allan Printing Ltd at their works
at Coombelands in Runnymede, England

Previous page:
Rearming a Spitfire V of No 312 (Czech) Squadron at Harrowbeer, July 1942.

Below:
Spitfire XVIs of No 403 (Canadian) Squadron at Evere, Belgium, in January 1945.
Public Archives of Canada

Front cover:
'The High Fighter'. The highest and longest combat ever flown over Britain, 12 September 1942.
From a painting by J. W. Mitchell, reproduced by kind permission of Mirage Fine Art

Introduction

My aim in writing my third volume in this series on the Spitfire, the best-known fighter aircraft of World War 2, has been to repeat the formula that has worked so well with previous volumes: to describe a series of incidents and to present little known documents that will be of interest to those whose interest in the Spitfire is just starting, while adding to the knowledge of those who have studied this aircraft over several years. Stiffening the text is a large number of previously unpublished photographs that will gladden the eye of the most ardent Spitfire buff.

The most famous action in which the Spitfire took part was, of course, the Battle of Britain whose 50th anniversary falls in 1990. The first chapter, 'Start of a Long Story', describes the test flying and career of the prototype Spitfire. 'Early Spitfires in Service' outlines the introduction of the Spitfire into service, in both the fighter and photographic reconnaissance roles. 'Spitfires in Captivity' runs to earth a little known aspect of the story: the Spitfires captured intact by the Luftwaffe prior to the Battle, some of which were used for propaganda photographs widely published at the time. The next chapter 'Battle of Britain Fighting Tactics', contains the document issued by the Tactics Branch of the Air Ministry in July 1940 outlining the tactics to be used by RAF fighters. 'Better Fitted for the Fight' describes the modifications which would give a significant improvement in the Spitfire's combat effectiveness during the Battle. In 'Battle of Britain Squadron Commander', Sqn Ldr Donald MacDonell describes his impressions as commander of No 64 Squadron during the initial part of the Battle. The next two chapters give the order of battle of Spitfire squadrons within Fighter Command on the evening of 14 September 1940, and a detailed analysis of the Spitfire in combat on 15 September.

Following the victorious conclusion of the Battle of Britain, the Spitfire began to spread its wings in roles beyond that of defensive fighter. 'Circus No 5 and After' describes an early offensive sweep over France that Howard Squire would never forget. Later in 1941 No 111 Squadron operated the fighter in a novel way, described by Peter Durnford in 'Spitfire Night Fighters'. 'A Fair Day's Work'

describes the missions flown on a typical day in 1941 by No 1 Photographic Reconnaissance Unit based at Benson. 'No 11 Group Tactical Memorandum No 14', issued early in 1942, showed the ways in which that force's tactics had evolved during the previous 18 months. In 'First Spitfires to Malta', Stanley Grant, Ray Honeybone and George Revell

describe their parts in the dramatic operation to deliver the first batch of these fighters to the beleaguered island. 'Battle in the Stratosphere' tells of the action over Southampton on 12 September 1942, between Emanuel Galitzine and Horst Goetz. 'More Spitfires in Captivity' tells the stranger-than-fiction story of the Spitfire re-engined with a Daimler-Benz

engine and test flown in Germany during 1943. In 'D-Day Top Cover Squadron', Don Nicholson describes some little-known operations by Spitfire Mk VIIs of No 131 Squadron during and after the invasion of Normandy. 'Gyro Gunsight – The Great Leveller' tells the story of the development and introduction into service of the gyro gunsight, a 'secret weapon' that helped Allied fighters to retain air superiority during the closing months of the war in the face of German jet fighters. Finally, to round off the story, in 'The Last of the Few' Tommy Handley describes the combat missions by Seafire Mk 47s of 800 Squadron during the early stages of the Korean War in 1950; with their end the Seafire passed out of first line service in the Royal Navy.

As well as the individuals named above, the author wishes to express his thanks to the following for their kindness in making available material for this book: Ray Sturtivant, Harry van der Meer, Peter Arnold, Zdenek Hurt, Tom Willis, Bernd Barbas, Manfred Griehl, Fritz Trenkle, Ole Nicolajsen, Winston Ramsey, Eric Adamson and Bill Brook and Dilip Sarkar. Thanks are also due to the staffs of the R. J. Mitchell Museum, The Royal Air Force Museum and the Fleet Air Museum.

Until the middle of the war, the mark numbers denoting modifications to RAF aircraft were given in roman numerals. From 1943 to 1948 all new aircraft and versions of aircraft carried arabic mark numbers, while the previously roman numbered mark designations remained in use. Very few aircraft types remained in service long enough for the change-over to cause problems, but one of those to go through each stage of transition was the Spitfire and its naval derivative the Seafire. As a convention in this book, Spitfire and Seafire marks up to XVI are given in roman numerals, and those of later versions are given in arabic numbers.

Alfred Price
Uppingham
Rutland, 1989

Below:
Spitfire PR IG, serial R7059, of the Photographic Reconnaissance Unit pictured at St Eval in 1941. This aircraft flew a low altitude 'dicing' mission to Brest late on the afternoon of 17 June 1941 (see page 45). This version was painted overall in a very pale shade of pink, just off-white, the optimum camouflage for taking photographs just below the base of the cloud. The window for the port-facing oblique camera is immediately to the right of the fuselage marking. Note the unusual position and style of the marking on the top surface of the wing; no markings were carried below the wings. *Green*

1 Start of a Long Story

The prototype aircraft, K5054, flew for the first time on 5 March 1936 from the Supermarine airfield at Eastleigh near Southampton with Vickers Chief Test Pilot Mutt Summers at the controls. At this time the aircraft was known only by its service specification number, F.34/37. It wore a bare metal finish with RAF markings on the wings and fuselage, and silver dope on the ailerons, elevators and rudder. For the maiden flight the aircraft was fitted with a fine-pitch propeller, the undercarriage fairings were not fitted and the main wheels were locked down.

Three days after its maiden flight K5054 took off on its second flight, this time with a coarse-pitch propeller, the undercarriage fairings in place and the main wheels unlocked and able to retract. During the days that followed, Summers, soon joined by Supermarine test pilots George Pickering and Jeffrey Quill, began to explore the performance envelope of the new fighter.

The initial flight test programme was completed early in April, and on the 10th the aircraft went into the hangar at Eastleigh for modifications. The flight tests had revealed that the rudder was over-

balanced, and to cure this the horn balance at the top of the rudder was reduced in area and the top of the fin was squared off to accommodate the change. Also the carburettor air intake under the nose was lowered a little, to increase the ram air pressure. The joints in the airframe were then filled in and carefully rubbed down, then the new fighter was painted overall in a pale blue colour scheme. At this time the fighter received its official name, 'Spitfire'. On 11 May the prototype resumed flying, and on the 26th it was delivered to Martlesham Heath for formal testing by

Believed taken shortly before the prototype K5054 made its first flight from Eastleigh on 5 March 1936, this photo shows the F.37/34 in its original unpainted condition.

Below:
In May 1936 the new fighter was officially named the Spitfire and that month it emerged from the hangar after initial modifications, painted in its light blue colour scheme.   *Smith*

Bottom:
Test pilot 'Mutt' Summers landing the prototype Spitfire at the Society of British Aircraft Constructors' display at Hatfield on 29 June 1936. For this and the RAF Pageant at Hendon two days earlier, the aircraft bore a '2' on the fuselage. Note the limited 60° travel of the flaps on the prototype aircraft, increased to 90° on production aircraft.

RAF pilots. From the start the new fighter created a favourable impression, and the service placed an immediate order for 310 Spitfires.

In March 1937 the prototype was damaged in a crash landing near Martlesham Heath, following an engine failure. When K5054 resumed flight testing, in the following September, the aircraft was painted in the standard RAF brown-and-green camouflage pattern and it wore this for the rest of its life.

By the end of October 1938 some 20 production Spitfires were flying and one of these replaced K5054 in the fighter's test programme. No longer required by the company, the prototype was sent to Farnborough in November for use in general perfomance testing. The aircraft continued in this role until 4 September 1939, the day after the outbreak of war, when it suffered severe damage in a landing accident in which the pilot, Flt Lt 'Spinner' White, was killed. K5054 was not repaired following this accident and parts of the airframe were used by the Photographic Department at Farnborough for the construction of the prototype camera installation for the Spitfire. Once that task was complete, the remains of the prototype were scrapped.

Right:
The cockpit of the prototype Spitfire, photographed late in 1936 or early in 1937. Note the random positioning of the flight instruments and the unusual type of gun firing button. *R. J. Mitchell Museum*

In September 1937 the prototype resumed flying following repairs, now wearing the standard green and brown RAF camouflage pattern of the period.

2 Early Spitfires in Service

The first unit to re-equip with the Spitfire was No 19 Squadron at Duxford, which received its first aircraft in August 1938. By the middle of December the unit had its full complement of aircraft and other units started to re-equip with the type. When the war broke out in September 1939 the RAF had accepted delivery of just over 300 Spitfires. Ten fighter squadrons (Nos 19, 41, 54, 65, 66, 72, 74, 60, 603 and 611) were operational with the type and one (No 609) was in the process of re-equipping.

Initially the precious Spitfires were issued only to home defence fighter units. With the coming of war, however, the RAF urgently needed a high performance photographic reconnaissance aircraft and a stripped down version of the fighter was proposed for the role. In October 1939 two Spitfires were modified as reconnaissance aircraft. The guns, radios and other items not considered strictly necessary were removed from the planes, and a vertical camera was installed in the gun bay in each wing. The aircraft were painted in the pale green 'Camotint' low visibility scheme overall, and then polished to give the last ounce of speed that was to be their sole protection from enemy fighters.

In November 1939 the reconnaissance Spitfires deployed to Seclin near Lille as part of No 2 Camouflage Unit, a deceptive title intended to conceal their true role. As more converted Spitfires became available the unit expanded, and early in 1940 it was re-designated No 212 Squadron. The unit flew numerous sorties during the hectic months of May and June 1940, and photographed each stage of the relentless advance of the German Panzer columns as they stormed through Belgium and France and on to the Channel coast. Throughout the Dunkirk evacuation the squadron continued to operate, cut off from the main British forces and withdrawing from airfield to airfield across central France. No 212 Squadron was the last RAF unit to leave France intact; its last two Spitfires were flown out on 14 June (10 days after Dunkirk fell) and the unit's ground personnel were flown out by transport aircraft, or evacuated by sea via the ports of La Rochelle and Bordeaux.

Below:
Spitfires of No 19 Squadron, the first unit to receive the new fighter.

Above:
K9987 of No 66 Squadron based at Duxford, the second unit to receive Spitfires, carrying the units's original RV identifcation code letters. On the starboard wing, just outboard of the root, is an early type combat camera.

Below:
First photo mission: this shot was taken at Seclin near Lille on 18 November 1939, during the preparations for the first photo reconnaissance sortie by a Spitfire. The aircraft, N3071 of No 2 Camouflage Unit, was one of two Mk Is whose guns were removed and had vertical cameras fitted in the gun bay in each wing. Flt Lt 'Shortie' Longbottom was to photograph the Siegfried Line defences in the Aachen area.

LAC Fred Hunt, the airman crouching under the starboard wing, served as an airframe fitter with the unit. He told the author that the so-called Camotint scheme worn by the aircraft was a delicate shade of very pale bluish-green which, under certain light conditions, appeared to have a pinkish tinge. On the ground this made the aircraft most conspicuous, but once it was airborne the Spitfire merged well into the sky background. 'The planes were very highly polished before every sortie. Much time was spent polishing them with wax furniture polish', he commented. Because of the considerable secrecy afforded these reconnaissance missions, most of the pre-flight preparations took place in the hangar. At the last moment the Spitfire was pushed outside and one of the ground crew ran the engine for a few minutes to warm it up. Then the engine was stopped, the tanks were filled to the top, the pilot got in and took off. When it landed after a mission, the Spitfire was immediately pushed into the hangar to get it out of sight.
Green

Right:
An aircraft of No 72 Squadron pictured in June 1940, fitted with 'blinkers' in front of the cockpit to shield the pilot's eyes from the glare of the exhaust flames.

Below:
Spitfire of No 41 Squadron during a re-deployment early in the war, with the Ensign transports that had assisted in the move.

Bottom:
Scene from one of the hangars at Drem, early in 1940. The four Spitfires on the right belong to No 602 Squadron. The aircraft on the right with no squadron identification letters is L1007, the prototype cannon-armed Spitfire, flying operational trials from the airfield at this time. *Cameron*

3 Spitfires in Captivity

The successful German offensive in the spring of 1940 culminated in the occupation of Holland, Belgium, Luxembourg and much of France. By its end the Luftwaffe possessed large numbers of foreign aircraft in a flyable or near flyable condition. Four of them were Spitfires.

The Spitfire received its baptism of fire while providing air cover for Allied troops retreating to, and being evacuated from, the area around Dunkirk. There was fierce fighting over the evacuation area, with heavy losses on both sides. In the course of the actions between 21 May and 4 June, more than 60 Spitfires were lost in action.

The first Spitfire to fall into German hands intact was K9867, ZP-J of No 74 Squadron. This aircraft forced landed at Calais-Marck airfield on 23 May, while the area was held by Allied troops. When German troops captured the airfield on 26 May, the Spitfire was still there.

For the Spitfire squadrons the worst single day during the Dunkirk evacuation was 1 June, when 12 aircraft were lost. One of those forced down, P9317/ZD-A of No 222 Squadron, made a wheels-down landing at Le Touquet airfield held by German troops.

Since November 1939 a few Spitfires modified for photographic reconnaissance had been operating from bases in France. In February 1940 these aircraft were incorporated into No 212 Squadron, with a detachment based at Seclin near Lille. No 212 Squadron flew throughout the Battle of France, and withdrew to England with most of its aircraft and personnel in June. It left behind one Spitfire intact, however: P9331, a PR 1B which had suffered a glycol leak during a mission on 7 June and landed at Rheims/Champagne. The aircraft was still there four days later when German troops captured the airfield.

The fourth Spitfire to fall intact into German hands had been the first of all to arrive in France: Spitfire 01, the 251st production aircraft, which had been delivered to the French Air Force in June 1939 for evaluation. This aircraft was at that Service's test centre at Orleans/Bricy when German troops overran the airfield on 18 June.

Thus, by the third week in June 1940, four Spitfires had fallen into German hands. We know that at least one of them was taken to the Luftwaffe test centre at Rechlin and made airworthy. Prior to the Battle of Britain, the fighter ace Hpt Werner Mölders test-flew both a Spitfire and a Hurricane. He later wrote:

'It was very interesting to carry out the flight trials at Rechlin with the Spitfire and the Hurricane. Both types are very simple to fly compared with our aircraft, and childishly easy to take-off and land. The Hurricane is very good-natured and turns well, but its performance is decidedly inferior to that of the Me109. It has strong stick forces and is "lazy" on the ailerons.

'The Spitfire is one class better. It handles well, is light on the controls, faultless in the turn and has a performance approaching that of the Me109. As a fighting aircraft, however, it is miserable. A sudden push forward on the stick will cause the motor to cut; and because the propeller has only two pitch settings (take-off and cruise), in a rapidly changing air combat situation the motor is either overspeeding or else is not being used to the full.'

Left:
The first Spitfire captured intact by German forces: K9867, ZP-J, of No 74 Squadron. This aircraft forced landed at Calais-Marck on 23 May 1940 when the airfield was held by Allied forces. It was still there three days later when the airfield was overrun. *Barbas*

Right:
The second Spitfire captured was P9317, ZD-A of No 222 Squadron, which made a forced landing at Le Touquet airfield held by German troops, on 1 June. *Barbas*

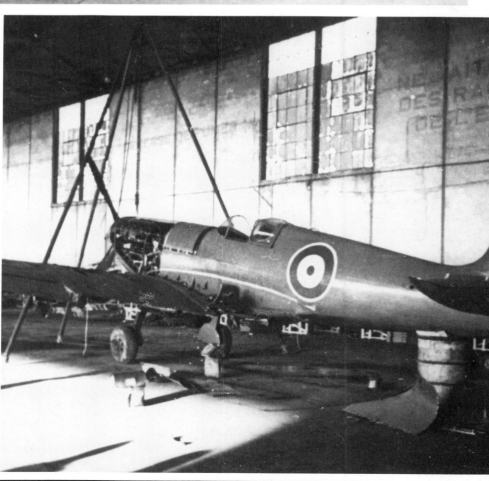

Mölders' remarks were probably not intended to be a fully objective assessment of the British fighter, but he put his finger on two weaknesses of the early Spitfires. At the time he made his remarks one of the weaknesses was in the process of being cured: under a crash programme all Spitfires in frontline units were being retro-fitted with constant speed airscrews, thus overcoming the problem of the earlier two-pitch propeller. The problem of the motor cutting out when the plane was bunted would be more difficult to cure, however, and would remain with the fighter for some time to come.

Oblt Hans Schmoller-Haldy of *Jagdgeschwader (JG) 54* also had the chance to fly a captured Spitfire at about this time, and he was rather more impressed with it as an adversary. He told the author:

'My first impression was that it had a beautiful engine. It purred. The engine of the Messerschmitt 109 was very loud. Also the Spitfire was easier to fly, and to land, than the Me109. The 109 was unforgiving of any inattention. I felt familiar with the Spitfire from the very start. That was my first and lasting impression. But with my experience with the 109, I personally would not have traded it for a Spitfire. It had the impression, though I did not fly the Spitfire long enough to prove it, that the 109 was the faster especially in the dive. Also, I think the pilot's view was better from the 109. In the Spitfire one flew further back, a bit more over the wing.

'For fighter-versus-fighter combat, I thought the Spitfire was better armed than the Me109. The cannon fitted to the 109 were not much use against enemy fighters, and the machine guns on top of the engine often suffered stoppages. The cannon were good if they scored a hit, but their rate of fire was very low. The cannon had greater range than the machine guns. But we were always told that in a dogfight one could not hope to hit anything at ranges greater than 50 metres, it was necessary to close in to short range.'

During the Battle of Britain at least two further Spitfires fell into German hands in a repairable condition: N3277, AZ-H of No 234 Squadron, which forced landed near Cherbourg on 15 August; and X4260,

XT-D of No 603 Squadron which belly landed near Guinnes on 6 September.

After the Battle of Britain two Spitfires, or one Spitfire repainted in two different sets of British markings, featured in a series of propaganda photographs taken by the Luftwaffe. One of these aircraft carried the spurious squadron code G-X and featured an unusual layout of roundels: Type B (red/blue) markings on the upper surface of the wings well inboard of the usual position, and larger Type B markings on the fuselage. The other Spitfire had Type B markings in the usual place on the upper wing surfaces, but featured oversized Type A1 (red/white/blue/yellow) markings on the fuselage and carried no squadron code letters.

It is difficult to establish with certainty the identities of the Spitfires flown in British markings by the Luftwaffe, though it is possible to state which they were not. One give-away is the radio mast: both Spitfires which appeared in the German photographs were fitted with the pointed mast introduced early in 1940. That rules out the first aircraft captured, K9867, and the French Spitfire 01, both of which were fitted with the early type cylindrical mast. And it rules out the photographic reconnaissance aircraft P9331, which had no radio mast at all. That reduces the list to P9317, N3277 and X4260, with P9317 as a most likely contender because she was the first one captured and with the least damage.

Above and below:
The fourth Spitfire captured intact by the Germans on 18 June 1940, was the sole aircraft of this type delivered to the French Air Force before the war. Designated No 01 in that service, it is pictured at the test centre at Orleans/Briecy. *Gentilli, Willis.*

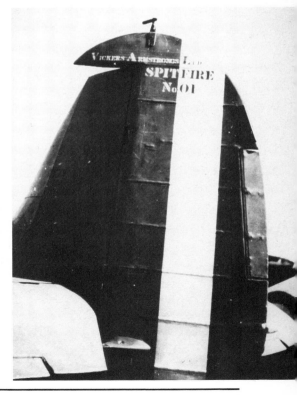

During the Battle of Britain at least two other Spitfires were forced down in France and captured intact.

Above and left:
N3277, AZ-H of No 234 Squadron, forced landed near Cherbourg on 15 August with battle damage immediately behind the cockpit. As can be seen, the damage was repaired and the aircraft repainted in German markings presumably in preparation for it to be test flown. *Trenkle, Griehl.*

Below:
X4260. XT-D of No 603 Squadron, made a wheels-up landing near Guinnes on 6 September. Later the undercarriage was lowered and the machine was taken to Guinnes airfield. *Barbas*

Left:
Further shots of XT-D. Later still at Guinnes, the aircraft was repainted in Luftwaffe markings presumably also prior to it being test flown. *Willis*

Below:
Early model Spitfire pictured at the Luftwaffe test centre at Rechlin. *Willis*

Right:
One of the captured Spitfires was repainted in British camouflage, with the spurious identification letters G-X and with wing roundels closer to the fuselage than normal. This aircraft featured in several propaganda photos.

Bottom:
G-X repainted in German markings some time after the propaganda photos were taken. The fitting under the rear fuselage might be a generator for smoke, to give the illusion that the aircraft was on fire. *via Petrick*

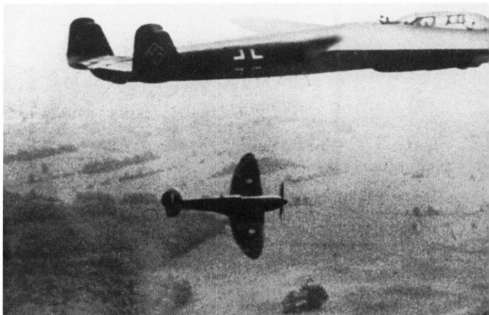

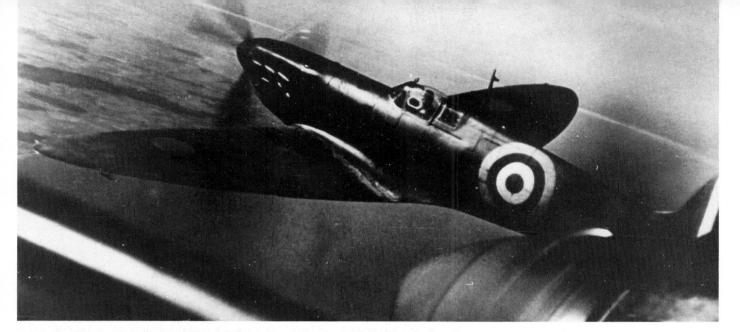

Above:
Another captured Spitfire, or perhaps G-X in another guise, can be identified by the lack of squadron identification letters and oversized fuselage roundels. This aircraft, too, featured in several propaganda shots. *via Willis*

Left:
As well as the single Spitfire delivered to the French government, three of these aircraft had been delivered to Turkey by June 1940. The fighters were operated by the 42 Av Bölük (4th Air Regiment) based at Corlu near Istanbul. This example, given the Turkish serial 2903, had previously been P9567. *Nicolajsen*

4 Better Fitted for the Fight

Between the outbreak of war and the start of the Battle of Britain, the Mark I version of the Spitfire underwent several detailed improvements to make it a more capable fighting aircraft. In this section we examine the changes, and their effects on the fighter's performance.

In the spring of 1940, in a bid to improve the performance of its fighters, the RAF introduced 100 octane petrol instead of the 87 octane fuel previously used. In the case of the Merlin IIs and IIIs fitted to the Spitfire I, this gave no improvement at or above the engines' full-throttle altitude set at 16,500ft. Below that altitude, however, the new fuel gave a valuable increase in power. Supercharger boost could be increased from +6½lb to +12lb without causing detonation in the cylinders, and this increased the maximum speed of the Spitfire by 25mph at sea level and 34mph at 10,000ft. Up to full-throttle height the fighter's climbing performance was also improved.

A further significant improvement in performance, in particular at take-off and in the climb, came with the installation of constant speed de Havilland or Rotol airscrews in place of the earlier two-pitch type: when fitted with one of the new propellers the Spitfire I's rate of climb was increased by about a half and the take-off distance was reduced by about a third.

Other modifications made to the Spitfire at this time, although they improved its fighting ability, detracted from performance. To protect the pilot and other vital parts of the plane, shaped steel plates were installed behind and beneath the pilot and in front of the fuel and glycol tanks; in total the sections of steel armour weighed 73lb. A thick slab of laminated glass was fitted on the front of the windscreen to protect the pilot's head and the sheet of light alloy covering the fuel tanks was thickened to 10SWG, about 3mm (sufficient to make rounds impacting at a shallow angle to ricochet off).

Another important addition was the installation of IFF (Identification Friend or Foe) transponder equipment. Although it imposed a weight and performance penalty, this equipment was essential to enable the aircraft to identify itself on the screens at radar stations along the coast of Great Britain, on which the RAF's fighter control system depended.

The various modifications added about 335lb to the Spitfire, and brought its all up weight to around 6,155lb. Moreover, some of the changes increased drag and so reduced the plane's top speed: for example, the slab of toughened glass mounted in front of the windscreen cost 6mph, the IFF wire aerials from the fuselage to the tip of each tailplane shaved off another 2mph. The maximum speed usually quoted for the Spitfire I is 362 mph at 18,5000 feet; but that figure referred to K9787, the first production aircraft with an all-up weight of 5,819lb. By the summer of 1940 the maximum speed of a fully equipped Mk 1 was somewhat lower, about 350mph, at the same altitude.

One further modification introduced before the Battle of Britain needs also to be mentioned here; and while it would give a significant improvement in the fighter's ability to manoeuvre effectively in combat, the weight and performance penalties were negligible.

During comparative flight tests of a captured Messerschmitt Bf109 against contemporary RAF fighters, it was discovered that in the German fighter the seat was more reclined than that in British fighters and the pilot could pull more 'G' without blacking out. To adjust the seating position in British fighters would have incurred a major modification programme, but a simpler solution was readily to hand. A Spitfire was modified with two-step rudder pedals, the lower step for normal flight and the upper step for use in high 'G' manoeuvres, ie in combat. Ft Lt Robert Stanford-Tuck of No 92 Squadron was asked to take the modified Spitfire through the repertoire of combat manoeuvres to determine the advantages and disadvantages of the modification. The questionnaire he was asked to fill in, and his answers to it, are reproduced right.

Right:
The cockpit of a Spitfire, showing the two-position rudder pedals on which Tuck commented so favourably.

Below:
Close-up of the laminated glass windscreen fitted to all fighter versions of the Spitfire before the Battle of Britain. Although the new windscreen gave valuable protection to the pilot's head from rounds coming from ahead, it lopped about 6mph off the top speed of the aircraft.

QUESTIONNAIRE ON AUXILIARY RUDDER PEDALS

You are requested after an extended and fair trial to express your views freely on the merits or disadvantages of the auxiliary rudder pedals.

Q1 Is the rudder easy to manipulate in manoeuvre using upper steps?
A1 Yes, comparatively so, as one only wants to use at higher speed and consequently very little rudder is required.

Q2 Have you proved that it raises your 'blacking out threshold' and enables you to do tighter turns.
A2 Yes, as when one is trying to shoot with heavy stresses on the body, the head can still be in the firing position relative to sight but knees are well up in the stomach, tightening muscles.

Q3 Is the upper step a comfortable position?
A3 For any period, definitely no. But for a short dogfight of, say, 20 minutes, it is not at all uncomfortable.

Q4 Is there any disadvantage in having the auxiliary step fitted?
A4 Absolutely none that I have found. It interferes in no way with any manoeuvres one might wish to do.

Q5 Any other comments?
A5 I have tried out these extra pedals over quite a long period now, and cannot find one single disadvantage in having them fitted, but on the other hand every advantage as outlined.

Station and date: PEMBREY 23.7.40
(signed) R. R. S. Tuck
F/Lieut

_____

On the strength of Tuck's recommendation, the two-step rudder pedals were installed in all new Spitfires and existing aircraft were fitted with them. During the Battle of Britain this relatively minor modification would enable Spitfire pilots to engage in manoeuvring combat more effectively than would otherwise have been the case.

5 Battle of Britain Fighting Tactics

The following paper, issued by the Air Tactics Branch of the Air Ministry in July 1940, was intended to familiarise fighter pilots with the lessons learned during the aerial fighting prior to the Dunkirk evacuation. As such, it was the most up-to-date tactical paper on air fighting available to Royal Air Force fighter pilots throughout the whole of the Battle of Britain period. The tactical paper provided a tactical framework within which pilots could make their own decisions in combat, and was not intended to lay down hard-and-fast rules.

HINTS AND TIPS FOR FIGHTER PILOTS

1 Most of our fighter experience in the war has been gained during the battles resulting from the invasion of Holland, Belgium and France. Under these conditions patrols were working either from aerodromes on the continent which were subjected to continual attacks and which had often to be evacuated, or from aerodromes in south-east England under improvised arrangements.

2 Some of the hints, therefore, are more applicable to such conditions than to home defence fighting, but they have been retained, because, although France has ceased to be a belligerent, and her aerodromes are closed to us, the distance between our own country and aerodromes occupied by the Germans is now so short that home defence operations are likely to have many of the features which we have been accustomed to connect only with continental operations. Such paragraphs have been marked with an asterisk.

Duties

3 Fighter pilots may be called upon for the following duties:

(a) *Home Defence* In this case fighters will be opposed to formations of enemy bombers usually escorted by fighters. Our patrols will normally be sent off to meet specific raids, the composition and strength of which may be known before interception takes place.

*(b) *Offensive Patrols over the Continent* These patrols will normally be despatched to areas in which enemy aircraft can be expected to be congregated. The strength and composition of the enemy forces will not be known before interception takes place. All types of enemy aircraft may be encountered.

(c) *Escort of Bomber or Reconnaissance Missions* In this case your duty is to ensure the safety of the aircraft which you are escorting and not to be drawn off in pursuit of aircraft which do not directly threaten them.

Enemy Formations

4 Although the enemy may adopt any type of formation, the following are those normally met:

(a) Bombers in vics of three, five or seven aircraft; vics in line astern, often stepped up to the rear or to the flank. Fighter escort is usually 3,000 to 4,000ft above and astern, or above and between the bombers and the sun. Fighters normally adopt a large vic formation of nine or twelve aircraft. One or more of these vics may be employed stepped up and behind each other.

(b) Bombers sometimes form a double vic, ie one vic inside another or a vic with one or more aircraft in the 'box' so as to give concentrations of defensive fire.

(c) Ju87 dive bombers are sometimes met with in no particular formation, particularly just before they deliver their attack. Under these conditions they form a large jumbled mass.

Defensive Tactics of Enemy Bombers

5 Enemy bombers when attacked may:

(a) close into tight formation;
(b) form a circle;
(c) if their formation is broken, dive to ground level and jink; or
(d) make for the nearest cloud;
(e) Ju88 has a habit of slowing up when attacked so that the fighter will over-run it and become a target for the rear guns of the Ju88.
(f) Sometimes also a flank aircraft of an enemy formation, which is not being engaged, will drop back to attack with cross fire a fighter attacking another aircraft of the formation.

Tactics of Enemy Escort

6 The enemy escorting fighters normally maintain their formation and position until our fighters start to attack the enemy bombers. Enemy fighters then immediately peel off in ones or twos in succession and dive very steeply upon our fighters. They open fire in the dive but do not usually attempt to remain on the tail of our fighters; instead, they continue their dive straight past and below and then climb up again into position for another attack.

Tactics to be Employed Against Enemy Formations

7 Fighters should never rush in to the attack of a formation immediately it is sighted. It is absolutely essential that the situation should be weighed up so that the most profitable method of attack can be decided upon, and also so that the disposition of the enemy fighters which are escorting the bombers may be studied. It must be remembered that the main aim is to shoot down the bombers; experience has proved that this cannot be done and that our fighters will be at a tactical disadvantage unless the enemy fighters are neutralised.

8 If, therefore, we have a strong force of fighters at least a quarter of them must be detached to take up the attention of the enemy fighters so that, while they are thus occupied, the remainder of our fighters can attack the enemy bombers without interruption.

9 If, however, our fighters are numerically inferior to the enemy escorting fighters, some form of stratagem must be employed. Suggested methods are:

(a) Attack or feint attack with small part of our force against the enemy fighters so as to draw them off.

(b) That the fighter should make a feint attack upon the bombers, thus bringing down the enemy fighters against him. Close watch should be kept upon the fighter as it dives and just before it arrives within range, its attack should be avoided by quick manoeuvre. Time may thus be gained for a very quick attack upon the bombers before the next fighter arrives within firing range.

(c) A detachment manoeuvres above or to the flank of the enemy fighters to give warning by R/T when enemy fighters start their attacking dive.

(d) Even a small detachment which reaches a position above the enemy fighters will often cause them to desert the bombers.

(e) If interference from enemy fighters can be temporarily neglected, a flight of five (*see para f*) aircraft can use the 'astern attack from the beam'. Aircraft take position in line astern, 800 yards to port of the enemy bomber formation, and ahead and 1,000 feet above, on the order 'turn to right in astern. Going down', the flight turns in simultaneously. Nos 1 and 2 deliver a full beam attack, Nos 3 and 4 a quarter attack, fighters break away to the left and downwards, reform line astern to port of the formation, and repeat the manoeuvre.

(f) Our fighters have generally attacked enemy bombers from astern. The introduction of armour in enemy bombers may force us to attack from the beam and even from directly ahead. Such attacks are more difficult to deliver but have been frequently adopted and when properly executed, have been extremely successful.

Don'ts

10 *(a)* Don't go into the middle of a vic of enemy bombers. If you do this they can concentrate the fire or their rear guns upon you. Attack them from the flank and if possible, from both flanks simultaneously.

(b) When you are going into the attack, don't give the enemy a chance of a deflection shot at you. As far as you can, keep your nose on the enemy, and approach in his blind spots as much as possible.

(c) Don't fire a long burst if enemy fighters are about; two seconds is long enough. Then break away quickly to ensure that an enemy fighter is not about to attack you. If all is clear, then you can immediately renew your attack upon the bomber.

(d) Don't break away by means of a climbing turn. This gives an easy shot to the enemy rear gunner. Break away outwards and downwards at as high a relative speed as possible.

(e) If the enemy forms a circle, don't attack it in a hesitating manner. When you attack a circle go straight into it without hesitation as soon as you can find a gap.

(f) Don't forget that enemy fighters can reach practically any part of this country. Never relax your vigilance.

Patrolling

11 *(a)* Make certain before leaving the ground that you thoroughly understand the orders for the patrol and what you are expected to do.

(b) If your patrol is ordered to take off at a fixed time, be ready in plenty

of time so that you can sit quietly and calmly in your aircraft, collecting your thoughts, before you have to take off.

(c) In choosing a height for your patrol, always try to patrol higher than the enemy.

(d) Never patrol in tight formation. Two-five spans is a comfortable distance which allows you to search around you without fear of collision.

(e) The rear aircraft or section of any fighter formation must always be in a position to watch the sky astern of the formation and to give warning of attacks by enemy fighters. If aircraft are in a single composite formation, the rear two aircraft should continually 'weave', ie swing across and exchange places with each other so that they can keep this watch to the rear. All aircraft in the formation, however, should try to assist in watching the whole sky.

(f) A useful patrol formation for a squadron is sections in line astern, stepped up, the third section to a flank and the rear section acting as look-out to the rear. Alternatively, aircraft have successfully patrolled in flights of five, each five forming an independent unit under its own leader. The look-out is provided by Nos 4 and 5 crossing over above the formation. On sighting the enemy formation, No 4 or

The photograph above, and those on the next two pages, depict Spitfires of No 602 Squadron during the Battle of Britain and were supplied by Dugald Cameron.

Above:
Flg Off Alistair Grant's aircraft, LO-H K9899, pictured at readiness at Drem.

5 dives down in front of the leader, indicating the position of the enemy by clock code over the R/T. As soon as he is in front of the formation, he turns off in the direction of the enemy. When the formation leader spots the enemy, he reassumes the leadership. If more than one flight of five operate together, No 1 flight takes position above and to the flank of No 2 Flight, each flight providing its own look-out.

(g) The same section should not be detailed to act as look-out for the whole period of the patrol because its 'weaving' tactics use up considerably more petrol than normal straight flying.

*(h) Don't patrol continuously along the same track. This will allow enemy fighters to anticipate your movements and obtain a favourable position for a surprise attack on you.

*(i) When patrolling, change your height and course continuously to avoid anti-aircraft fire.

(j) If you are patrolling, as you should, with a portion of your force

acting as an upper guard, this guard should regulate its movements so that it can immediately go to the assistance of the lower formation when required.

(k) Never leave your formation unless ordered to do so.

Enemy Decoy Tactics

*12 If you see a lone bomber apparently without any particular employment, he will almost certainly be a decoy, and fighters, 4,000 feet above and probably hidden in the sun, are waiting for you to attack him. A favourite trick of enemy fighters is to allow one or two of their number to lead you just under clouds. When they have got you in that position, enemy fighters in superior numbers dive out of the clouds to attack you.

13 Always expect that enemy fighters are in the offing and are waiting for you to take some unguarded action.

Enemy Fighter Tactics

14 Me109s and Me110s normally fly in squadron formations of twelve.

15 Enemy fighters always like to be in superior numbers and to have the advantage of height and sun.

16 Unless they have these advantages, they will not usually stay to fight, but will make a quick diving attack hoping they have you at a disadvantage and will then use their speed to escape.

17 German fighters often work in pairs. If you get on the tail of one, the other immediately tries to get on your tail.

18 When attacked, German fighters will very often dive vertically away from you. It is not usually worthwhile to follow them especially if they are faster in the dive than you are. If you are over German territory he may try to lead you over a FLAK battery.

19 The Me110, after he has attacked, will often pull up into a stall turn, so that he may have a look round to see where he should go next. If you can catch him at the top of his zoom, he is very easily shot down.

20 The Me110 will often make a head-on attack at you, and open fire with cannons at long range. He does not like to hold on to this attack to close range.

Dogfight Hints

21 *(a)* Formations quickly become broken up in a dogfight. Aircraft of sections should try, as far as possible, to keep together for mutual support.

(b) If you hear the sound of firing, turn immediately. The sound almost certainly comes from an enemy fighter which is attacking you from astern.

(c) Turn sharply and slightly downwards. Hurricanes and Spitfires are more manoeuvrable than German fighters and they will have difficulty following you in your turn. The Me109 is particularly bad at a sharp turn to the right.

(d) If you are involved in a head-on attack, remember the rule of the air: when you have to break away to avoid collision, turn to the right.

(e) Never waste ammunition. The golden opportunity may come when your ammunition is finished.

(f) Be especially careful at the moment you break off a combat. Take evasive action immediately because you are especially liable to attack at this moment. A useful manoeuvre to break off a combat is a dive using full aileron. Regain height as soon as possible.

(g) If your engine stops dive straight down to make the enemy think that he has 'got' you. Manoeuvre without engine gives the game away, and the enemy likes to concentrate on the 'lame duck'.

(h) If you have to bail out, half-roll on to your back, open the lid, undo your straps and push the stick forward.

(i) Never fly straight, particularly if you are alone. Keep continually turning from side to side so that you can keep a look-out behind you. If the sun is bright and is behind you, it is advisable to make a 360-deg turn at short intervals so that you can make quite certain that the sky is clear in all directions.

(j) **Beware of the Hun in the Sun.**

Night Fighting

22 The object in night fighting is to 'stalk' the enemy and to reach firing position without being observed. The following points should be noted:

(a) Under normal conditions of darkness, aircraft which are not illuminated by searchlights can best be spotted when they are between 40-deg and 60-deg above you.

(b) Cockpit and instrument lighting should be reduced to the barest minimum to assist you in searching for the enemy, and to prevent your own presence being revealed.

(c) The illuminated ring sight should be dimmed so it is only just visible.

(d) Before opening fire the aircraft must be positively identified as an enemy. This is best achieved from a position below him.

(e) The following method of attack is recommended by Fighter Command. Having reached a position below the enemy and regulated your speed to his, slightly raise the nose of your aircraft without increasing the throttle opening; you will thus rise behind the enemy. Keep below his slipstream — if you have difficulty in holding your aircraft out of the slipstream it is usually an indication that you have reached too great a range.

(f) The range at which the enemy is engaged should be as short as possible; in no circumstances should it be greater than 150 yards.

Above:
Spitfire at 15min readiness at Westhampnett. *via Cameron*

General Hints

23 *(a)* If there is a chance that enemy fighters may be about, look well before you take off, turn quickly, be especially careful while circling the aerodrome before landing and don't make a long straight approach.

(b) Light AA guns from the ground are accurate and effective up to 4,000 feet. The most dangerous heights for heavy AA guns are between 4,000 and 8,000 feet.

(c) Watch that your oxygen fittings do not come adrift.

(d) Don't leave your transmitter on 'send'. If you do, you make communication impossible for the whole formation and you may ruin the patrol.

(e) Remember to turn on your sight, and cine-camera, if you have one.

(f) If you have been in action, test your hydraulic system for possible damage before you get back to your home aerodrome.

(g) If you see white or greyish smoke pouring out of an engine of the enemy aircraft, it probably means that you have damaged his cooling or oil circulation. You should therefore switch your aim to the other engine. Black smoke may indicate either that the engine has been damaged or that the pilot is overboosting. There are

indications that the enemy will try to produce smoke artificially so as to deceive you, so you must use your judgement as to whether you have caused sufficient damage to make it impossible for him to return to his base.

(h) If you are in a single-seater and have to land in the sea, bail out if possible; if you cannot, take the following action on the way down:

(i) Open cockpit cover and lock in open position.

(ii) Release oxygen and R/T fittings.

(iii) Release parachute harness. DON'T undo Sutton Harness.

(iv) See that flotation waistcoat is only very lightly inflated. If it is fully inflated its buoyancy may prevent you escaping.

(v) Just before you touch the water, take two or three deep breaths.

(vi) As soon as the shock of touching the water has ceased, undo Sutton Harness and heave yourself out of the cockpit.

(vii) Blow up flotation waistcoat as soon as you reach the surface.

Finally

24 Remember that the closer the range, the more certain you are of bringing down the enemy. Remember also that everyone tends to under-estimate range and that when you think you are within 200 yards of the enemy you are probably still 400 yards away.

6 Battle of Britain Squadron Commander

Donald MacDonell joined the Royal Air Force in 1932, and trained as a pilot at Cranwell. After receiving his commission he was posted to No 54 Squadron equipped with Bristol Bulldogs. In 1935 he was seconded to the Fleet Air Arm and flew Nimrod fighters from the aircraft carriers Courageous *and* Glorious. *In 1937 he qualified as a flying instructor, and the following year was posted as a flight commander to the flying school at Drem. In 1939 he was promoted to squadron leader and posted to the Directorate of Training in the Air Ministry. In July 1940, when the Battle of Britain was in its opening stages, he was appointed officer commanding No 64 Squadron at Kenley equipped with Spitfire Is.*

When MacDonell assumed command of No 64 Squadron, the unit was flying daily patrols to escort convoys passing through the Straits of Dover. With increasing frequency the Spitfires encountered Junkers Ju87 dive bombers escorted by Messerschmitt Bf109s, but although the squadron's pilots had several close shaves and some of its aircraft suffered damage, the unit went through most of July without the loss of a single aircraft or pilot.

All of that changed on the afternoon of the 25th, however, during the series of hard-fought actions over Convoy CW8 off Folkestone. At the head of his squadron, MacDonell reached the convoy as the Junkers Ju87s of II Gruppe of Sturzkampf-geschwader 1 completed an attack on the ships and were heading south at low altitude in a gaggle. Coming down fast, the Spitfires closed rapidly on their prey:

'I picked out one of the Stukas and went after it. The German rear gunner was firing back and I felt a "thump" as my Spitfire was hit. Then I opened up at him with my eight guns. As my rounds struck home, bits fell off the Stuka then suddenly it rolled on its back and dived into the sea.'

Its glycol system damaged, the Spitfire headed back to Hawkinge with a badly overheating engine. The redoubtable Merlin kept going until the fighter was passing over the airfield boundary, then it finally packed up. MacDonell was able to make a normal landing. During the action

Above:
Sqn Ldr Donald MacDonell, commander of No 64 Squadron during the Battle of Britain.
MacDonell

No 64 Squadron lost two Spitfires: the pilot of one was killed, that of the other suffered injuries from which he later died.

In a similar action four days later MacDonell gained his second victory, again a Junkers Ju87, followed a few minutes later by a Messerschmitt Bf109. One of the unit's Spitfires suffered damage during this engagement.

In time of war a fighter squadron is a close-knit unit, and MacDonell found that among pilots the attitude towards rank was quite different from that he had known before the war:

'In wartime, it was inevitable that democracy should creep into a small fighting unit like a Spitfire squadron. Having been in the Service since 1932, at first I found it strange to hear the NCO pilots calling junior officer pilots by their Christian names or nicknames. I did not stop it – the most important thing was to maintain morale.

'Among the pilots discipline was a bond, self-imposed by a common purpose. I was the only "Sir" on the squadron.

'That sort of democracy was restricted to the aircrew, however. The NCO groundcrew had been in the Service a long time and they maintained the old standards. They served their pilots with a technical and emotional devotion which was quite outstanding.'

In wartime, fighter formations were led by the most experienced pilot, regardless of his rank:

'Flying experience was what mattered most. On one occasion I had to go to Group Headquarters, one of the Flight Commanders was on leave and the squadron was suddenly ordered to move from Leconfield to Wittering. A flight sergeant was the most experienced pilot available, so he led the squadron. That would never have happened in peace time.'

August brought hectic activity for the squadron, with numerous combat scrambles and long periods at readiness in between. MacDonell was credited with the destruction of two Bf109s on the 5th, another on the 8th, one on the 11th and two more on the 15th. No 64 Squadron's days settled into a routine, if 'routine' is the appropriate word for a period in which death or the risk of death was ever-present.

At Kenley, No 64 Squadron's dispersal area was at the north of the airfield, at the opposite side from the hangars and administrative buildings. The Spitfires were parked in the E-shaped earth-and brick revetments beside the perimeter track, and from time to time the ground crews would start the engines of the planes at readiness to warm the oil and ensure they could take off immediately.

'When we were at readiness the pilots would be relaxing at the dispersal area – reading, chatting, playing cards. Each Flight had a separate crew room, so no pilot was too far from his Spitfire. I would be out of my office, wearing flying kit and Mae West, with the Flight I was to lead on that day. Each pilot's parachute was laid out on the seat of his aircraft, with the straps laid over the armour plating at the back of the cockpit.

'Every time the telephone rang there would be a ghastly silence. The orderly would answer it and one would hear something like: "Yes, Sir . . . Yes, Sir . . . Yes, Sir . . . Sgt Smith wanted on the phone." And everyone would breath again.'

If the call was for the squadron to scramble, the orderly would should 'SCRAMBLE!' at the top of his voice and every pilot would dash for his plane:

'By the time I reached my Spitfire the mechanic would have started the engine. He got out of the cockpit and I got in, and he helped me strap into my parachute. Then he passed the seat straps and helped me fasten them. When I gave the thumbs up he would shut the side door, jump to the ground and run round in front of the port wing. Meanwhile I tightened my various straps, pulled on my helmet and plugged in the R/T lead. After checking that the engine was running properly, I would wave the groundcrew to pull away the chocks, open the throttle, and move forward out of my blast pen.

'After a fast taxi across the grass to the take-off position I would line up, open the throttle wide and begin my take-off run. The rest of my pilots followed me as fast as they could. The whole thing, from the scramble order to the last aircraft leaving the ground, took about a minute and a half.

'As soon as we were off the ground and climbing, I would inform operations "Freema Squadron airborne" ["Freema" was No 64 Squadron's radio callsign]. The Sector Controller would come back and tell me where he wanted me to go and at what altitude. While the squadron was forming up I would climb in a wide spiral at low boost, until everyone was in place. Then I would open up to a high throttle setting to get to altitude as fast as possible. In the spiral climb I would always edge to the north; the enemy formations always came from the south or southeast, and it was important to avoid climbing below the enemy's fighter cover. As well as keeping watch for the enemy, I would be watching the station-keeping of my squadron. If anyone was beginning to straggle I would throttle back a little.'

With the long periods on standby, flying two, three or more operational scrambles each day and sometimes a night patrol as well, by nightfall the pilots were usually extremely tired.

Between 25 July and 15 August the squadron lost five Spitfires and five pilots – two killed, two wounded and one taken prisoner. Their replacements came from the training schools and MacDonell had the task of preparing them for action:

'During the Battle of Britain one had to take every opportunity to train new pilots. Young pilots would arrive on the squadron with only six or seven hours' flying time on the Spitfire. One or two practice sorties could make all the difference to their ability to survive in combat. When we were at 30 minutes available, I might ring operations and ask permission to take one of the new pilots into the air for "follow my leader" practice. If one could take them up one could point out their failings and tell them: "You won't survive 10 minutes in battle if you fly like that!" The object was to tell them why and lead them round, not to frighten them.'

No 64 Squadron was heavily engaged on the 16th, and MacDonnell was shot down.

'We had been sent up against a raid by 50 or 60 Heinkel 111s, with a free-hunt of Messerschmitt 109s in front and a close escort of Messerschmitts above. There was a certain amount of cloud at about 8,000ft. We have been scrambled late, and broke cloud to find ourselves beneath and behind the Heinkels, which had turned round after dropping their bombs. I split my squadron, and told the other flight to attack the bombers from the starboard side. I went in with my wing man, intending to attack the bombers from below and do as much damage as we could.

'We got in very close to the Heinkels and knocked one down, then we attacked two others and clearly damaged them. Then we were out of ammunition. There was a tremendous return fire from the bombers, so we broke off and dived for cloud. But by then the covering Messerschmitts were charging after us and just before we reached the cloud there was a frightful crash as my Spitfire was hit. The aircraft went out of control and I was forced to bail out. The Spitfire flown by my No 2, Plt Off P. Simpson, took eight hits from cannon shells but he managed to get it back to Kenley (later that aircraft was put on a low-loader and sent around the aircraft factories, to show workers how much punishment a Spitfire could take and still get home.)

'I came down in the garden of a little cottage near Uckfield, about a mile from where my Spitfire crashed. I released the parachute and was wandering around, when from an Anderson shelter there emerged a very frightened householder pointing a 12-bore shotgun at me. Then his wife came out of the shelter and said "I think he's one of ours, darling".'

Once it was clear MacDonell was not an enemy, he was taken into the house and given a large brandy.

At this time the German offensive against Fighter Command's airfields and radar stations was in full swing. Two days later, on 18 August, Kenley was attacked. As the raiders came in over the coast, eight Spitfires of No 64 Squadron were scrambled and ordered to patrol over base at 20,000ft. They were in position when suddenly the Kenley Sector Controller, Sqn Ldr Anthony Norman, called over the radio 'Bandits overhead!'. To MacDonell the warning sounded rather odd:

'Instinctively I looked up, but there was only the clear blue sky above. I thought "My God! Where are they?" Then I looked down and could see bombs bursting on the airfield. Realising the enemy planes were below us, I gave a quick call: "Bandits below. Tally Ho!" Then down we went in a wide spiral at high speed, keeping a wary eye open for the inevitable German fighters.'

Left:
Kenley airfield under attack from low-flying Dorniers, 18 August 1940. The Spitfire in the revetment, belonging to No 64 Squadron, suffered minor damage.

Above:
The Messerschmitt Bf110 flown by Oblt Rüdiger Proske of *I Gruppe Zerstörergeschwader 26*, shot down by Donald MacDonell on 18 August, pictured after it crash-landed near Lydd.

Kenley had been attacked by a small force of Dorniers running in at low altitude; that had been the reason for the odd-sounding radio call.

As the descending Spitfires reached 15,000ft they passed a formation of Dornier Do17s surrounded by a *mêlée* of Hurricanes and Messerschmitt Bf110s. These Dorniers were in the process of turning for home, having released their bombs on Kenley in a high altitude attack coordinated with the earlier one from low altitude.

'There was an awful lot going on, with aircraft flying in all directions. As we were descending, a squadron of Hurricanes came past us going towards the Dorniers. There was a lot of R/T chatter, too much, everybody was very excited.

'I dived beneath one of the enemy aircraft, which I took to be a Dornier, and pulled up to attack it from astern and underneath. I opened fire from about 300 yd. The starboard engine was hit, then the port engine emitted puffs of black smoke. I though the pilot had been hit, or the elevators damaged, because the aircraft stood on its tail, stalled, then went into a spin. I remember thinking "How amazing, that an aircraft can stall so soon after its engines were damaged". Rather foolishly I hung around, spellbound, watching it go down. Then I realised that there were better things to do, and pulled away. I did not see it crash but there was a lot of smoke and I didn't think it would get very far.'

In fact the 'Dornier' was a Messerschmitt Bf110 of *Zerstörergeschwader 26,* piloted by Oblt Rüdiger Proske. The speed and angle of MacDonell's approach had taken the German crew by surprise and Proske was unaware of the Spitfire's presence until his aircraft shuddered under the impact of hits. The accurate burst damaged both of the Messerschmitt's engines and wounded the rear gunner. In no position to fight back, the German pilot decided to 'play dead'; he released the stick and let the plane fall out of control. It was a convincing demonstration, as MacDonell testifies. Proske let the Messerschmitt spin through 6,000ft then, seeing that no British fighter was following, he regained control, levelled out and headed for the coast. Both of his engines were losing power however, and just short of the coast first one then the other juddered to a stop. The German pilot made a wheels-up landing on farmland near Lydd.

While Proske was limping away from Kenley, MacDonell was again in action, He found a Junkers Ju88 which had become separated from its formation, and made two firing runs on it before his ammunition ran out. The last he saw of the bomber, it was emitting smoke from the port engine and was under attack by a Hurricane. Almost certainly this was the bomber which came under attack from several British fighters that afternoon, and which crashed soon afterwards near Sevenoaks.

The co-ordinated attack on Kenley by low-flying and high-flying Dorniers had inflicted severe damage, and the station's fighter squadrons were ordered to land elsewhere.

'We received the order "Pancake Bye-Bye One" (Bye-Bye was the codename for the emergency landing grounds, which had refuelling and rearming facilities). Bye-Bye One was Redhill, and five of us landed there. I was worried about our three other planes – I thought they had come to grief. The Spitfires were rapidly refuelled but rearming was another matter – at the landing ground they had plenty of ammunition but it was not belted-up.

'After about half-an-hour I phoned Kenley operations and told them the aircraft were refuelled, but it would take the rest of the war to get them re-armed! They told us to return to Kenley, taking care to avoid the bomb craters. When we arrived we saw the three missing Spitfires, they had all landed safely.'

Only one of No 64 Squadron's aircraft suffered damage that day, caused by a bomb which exploded near the revetment in which it was parked.

On the next day, 19 August, No 64 Squadron left Kenley and moved to Leconfield in Yorkshire to rest, re-form and complete the training of its replacement pilots. At the end of October the unit returned south, this time to Biggin Hill. By then the Battle of Britain was in its closing stages, however, and there was little further action. On 11 November MacDonell engaged a Bf109 and reported having damaged it. On the 29th he engaged another of these fighters and shot it down, MacDonell's final kill during the battle, that brought his victory score to 11½.

On 13 March 1941, while leading his squadron as top cover for a daylight raid by Blenheims in the Pas de Calais area, Donald MacDonell was shot up by a Bf109. He managed to get halfway across the Channel, but then his engine seized and he was forced to bail out. After about half-an-hour in the sea he was picked up virtually unconscious by a German patrol boat and taken to Le Havre. He spent the remainder of the conflict as a prisoner of war.

7 Fighter Command Spitfire Units, 14 September 1940

This section gives the order of battle of operational Spitfire units in RAF Fighter Command at 6pm on the evening of 14 September 1940. The following day would see the climax of the Battle of Britain. To provide a full picture of Fighter Command's strength, Spitfires held in reserve in maintenance units, those serving with operational training units and the number produced during the preceding week are also included. The first figure denotes aircraft serviceable, unserviceable aircraft in parentheses.

NO 10 GROUP, HQ BOX, WILTSHIRE

Middle Wallop Sector
No 609 Squadron 15 (3) Middle Wallop
No 152 Squadron 17 (2) Warmwell

St Eval Sector
No 234 Squadron 16 (1) St Eval

Group Total   48 (6)

NO 11 GROUP, HQ UXBRIDGE, MIDDLESEX

Biggin Hill Sector
No 72 Squadron 10 (7) Biggin Hill
No 92 Squadron 16 (1) Biggin Hill
No 66 Squadron 14 (2) Gravesend

Hornchurch Sector
No 603 Squadron 14 (5) Hornchurch
No 41 Squadron 12 (6) Rochford
No 222 Squadron 11 (3) Rochford

Tangmere Sector
No 602 Squadron 15 (4) Westhampnett

Group Total   92 (28)

NO 12 GROUP, HQ WATNALL, NOTTINGHAMSHIRE

Duxford Sector
No 19 Squadron 14 (0) Fowlmere

Coltishall Sector
No 74 Squadron 14 (8) Coltishall

Wittering Sector
No 266 Squadron 14 (5) Wittering

Digby Sector
No 611 Squadron 17 (1) Digby

Kirton-in-Lindsey Sector
No 616 Squadron 14 (4) Kirton-in-Lindsey
No 64 Squadron 7 (3) Leconfield
                6 (3) Ringway

Group Total   86 (24)

NO 13 GROUP, HQ NEWCASTLE, NORTHUMBERLAND

Catterick Sector
No 54 Squadron 15 (2) Catterick

Usworth Sector
No 610 Squadron 14 (5) Acklington

Turnhouse Sector
No 65 Squadron 15 (5) Turnhouse

Group Total   44 (12)

Spitfires at Operational Training Units – 14 September: 26 (24)
Spitfire Production During Week Prior to 14 September: 38
Spitfires Held at Maintenance Units – 14 September:
Ready for Immediate Use 47
Ready in Four Days   10

8 The Spitfire in Action, 15 September 1940

On the evening of 14 September Fighter Command's Spitfire squadrons possessed 270 serviceable aircraft, plus a further 70 that were unserviceable. The Hurricane squadrons possessed 509 serviceable aircraft (plus 95 unserviceable). Thus Spitfires made up just over 34% of the Command's force of modern single-engined day fighters. The average serviceability of the Spitfires was 79%, that of the Hurricanes was 84%.

A major factor in Fighter Command's success during the large-scale engagements on 15 September was the exemplary performance of the RAF fighter control organisation. During the engagement around noon, against a raid on London, eight squadrons of Spitfires and 15 squadrons of Hurricanes were scrambled; all except one squadron of Hurricanes made contact with the enemy. During the second and much larger attack on London that afternoon, 10 squadrons of Spitfires and 18 squadrons of Hurricanes were scrambled; all made contact with the enemy.

Spitfires from 11 squadrons went into action on 15 September: Nos 19, 41, 66, 72, 92, 152, 222, 602, 603, 609 and 611 Squadrons. But significantly, eight Spitfire squadrons would not see action on that day: Nos 54, 64, 65, 74, 234, 266, 610 and 616 Squadrons. The latter were assigned to Nos 10, 12 and 13 Groups, responsible for the defence of the west and north of the country, and were based too far from the capital to go into action in its defence.

In the course of the day's fighting eight Spitfires were lost out of 192 sorties that engaged the enemy, a loss rate of 4.2%. Twenty-one Hurricanes were lost out of 327 sorties that engaged, giving a loss rate of 6.4%. Thus a Spitfire that made contact with the enemy was 66% more likely to survive such contact than a Hurricane. Nine out of 184 returning Spitfires had battle damage (4.8%), as did 23 out of 316 returning Hurricanes (7.2%). Compared with the Hurricane, the Spitfire's superior performance made it a more difficult opponent for enemy fighters and its smaller size made it less likely to take hits from the bombers' return fire.

During the two main engagements under consideration, 55 German aircraft were destroyed. One of the German planes appears to have been lost to accidental causes. Ground anti-aircraft fire was a contributory factor in four of the losses, though in each case fighters also had a

share in the victory. Of the 50 German planes that fell to fighter attack, many were attacked by both Spitfires and Hurricanes. As a result it is not possible to draw valid conclusions from this action regarding the relative merits of the Spitfire and the Hurricane as destroyers of enemy aircraft. On the average, one German aircraft was shot down for every 10 Spitfires and Hurricanes that made contact with the enemy.

During the day there were numerous violent and confused combats between the opposing fighters in the area east of London. Few of these manoeuvring combats lasted more then about 20sec, however: any pilot concentrating his attention too long on one enemy fighter ran the risk of being blasted out of the sky by another. On this day the author has found only *one* recorded instance of a protracted combat between individual fighters. Sqn Ldr Brian Lane commanded No 19 Squadron with Spitfires, part of Douglas Bader's Wing. When the Wing was split up Lane was attacked by a Bf109, he avoided the enemy fire then curved after the Messerschmitt to deliver his riposte:

'He saw me as I turned after him and, putting on full inside rudder as he turned, skidded underneath me. Pulling round half-stalled, I tore after him and got in a short burst as I closed on him before he was out of my sights again. That German pilot certainly knew how to handle a 109 – I have never seen one thrown about as that

one was, and felt certain that his wings would come off at any moment. However, they stayed on, and he continued to lead me a hell of a dance as I strove to get my sights on him again. Twice I managed to get in a short burst but I don't think I hit him, then he managed to get round towards my tail. Pulling hard round I started to gain on him and began to come round towards his tail. He was obviously turning as tightly as his kite could. I could see that his slots [on the leading edge of the wings] were open, showing he was nearly stalled. His ailerons were obviously snatching too, as first one wing and then the other would dip violently.

'Giving the Spitfire best, he suddenly flung out of the turn and rolled right over on his back passing across in front of me inverted. I couldn't quite see the point of his manoeuvre unless he hoped I would roll after him, when, knowing no doubt that my engine would cut [due to the float-type carburettor fitted to the Merlin engine] whereas his was still going owing to his petrol injection system, he would draw away from me. Either that or he blacked out and didn't realise what was happening for a moment, for he flew on inverted for several seconds, giving me the chance to get in a good burst from the quarter. Half righting himself for a moment, he slowly dived down and disappeared into the clouds still upside down, looking very much out of control.

'The sweat was pouring down my face and my oxygen mask was wet and sticky about my nose and mouth. I felt quite exhausted after the effort and my right arm ached from throwing the stick around the cockpit. At speed it needs quite a bit of exertion to move the stick quickly and coarsely in violent manoeuvres.'

Afterwards, Lane would claim the Bf109 'probably destroyed'. This claim does not link with any known German loss, however, and no Bf109 came down on land within 20 miles of Dartford where the combat was reported to have taken place.

As has been said, long manoeuvring combats were a rarity. More usually, fighter pilots engaging their enemy counterparts would follow the adage 'get in fast, hit hard, get out'.

No description of the activities of the Spitfire on 15 September 1940 would be complete without mention of the aircraft of the Photographic Reconnaissance Unit based at Heston, a squadron-sized unit charged with keeping track of the German invasion preparations. On that day the reconnaissance Spitfire, flying alone and carrying cameras and extra fuel instead of guns, photographed nearly every significant port between Antwerp in the east and Cherbourg in the west.

The converted fighters returned with a wealth of new intelligence. Their photographs of Antwerp revealed 16 merchant ships, six of them new arrivals, tied up at the quayside. At Zeebrugge were seven large merchant ships, and off-shore were 15 tugs and 30 barges. At Flushing an armada of about 150 barges had been assembled. A passenger ship escorted by four torpedo boats was photographed passing east of Calais. At Boulogne the photographs revealed 120 invasion barges and 150 small craft, an increase of 30 barges since the previous reconnaissance. Approaching Le Treport were 35 small motor boats. At Cherbourg there were five destroyers, six torpedo boats, nine minesweepers, four fast patrol boats and 15 merchant vessels. If anyone doubted it, here was evidence a-plenty that Adolf Hitler was serious in his intention to invade England.

Above and right:
No account of the work of the Spitfire during the Battle is complete without mention of the work of the Photographic Reconnaissance Unit at Heston, which maintained a close watch on the German invasion deployments. The main workhorse of the unit, the Spitfire PR IC, carried no guns and was fitted with cameras in the blister under the starboard wing and fuel in a similar blister under the port wing.

9 Circus No 5 and After

At the beginning of 1941 the RAF began its campaign of daylight attacks on targets in occupied France and Belgium, by light bombers with large forces of escorting fighters: Operation 'Circus'. Typical of the early operations of this type was Circus No 5, on the afternoon of 26 February 1941.

The target for Circus No 5 was harbour installations at Calais, to be attacked by 12 Blenheims of No 139 Squadron. The bombers crossed the French coast in formation at 17,000ft, their close escort comprising No 1 Squadron's Hurricanes flying slightly above, No 601 Squadron's Hurricanes a few thousand feet higher and No 303 Squadron's Spitfires at 22,000ft. The high cover wing comprised three Spitfire squadrons: No 74 at 24,000ft, and Nos 92 and 609 Squadrons at 26,000ft. This array of air power was sufficient to deter the German fighter force and although some Messerschmitts were seen airborne, none made any serious attempt to engage. The bombers completed their attack without interference and they and their escorts withdrew without loss.

Twenty minutes behind the main formation came the Spitfires of Nos 54 and 64 Squadrons, briefed to carry out a sweep between Dover and Cap Gris Nez at 28,000ft and engage enemy fighters drawn up by the earlier incursion. This time there were some skirmishes with Messerschmitts, though no Spitfire pilot made any claim. One Spitfire of No 54 Squadron was shot down however, that flown by Sgt Howard Squire. This is his story of that day:

'We were flying top cover, it was rather a hazy day and I saw nothing of the rest of the force or the coast of France. We were in two finger-fours – "B" Flight in front led by Flt Lt George Gribble and "A" Flight behind led by Flg Off Ray Charles. I was at the rear of "A" Flight, flying wing to Flg Off Chapman.

'When we were roughly over the coast of France an aircraft suddenly flashed past my nose, in a steep dive from left to right. It came past so quickly I did not recognise the type. My first thought was that it might be a decoy, to lure us down after it. An aircraft on its own suddenly appearing like that would not have been a mistake; it was there for a purpose.

'Nobody spoke on the radio, but suddenly Chapman pealed after the diving plane. That was a stupid thing to do and I hesitated briefly before following him – but my job was to guard his tail. The delay would be my undoing. Had I followed immediately, we would at least have kept

Below:
The afternoon of 26 February 1941: a prisoner of the Luftwaffe, Sgt Howard Squire is entertained at the Officers' Mess at Calais-Marck. *Djoud*

together. But the delay put him that bit further in front of me, and almost immediately I lost sight of him against the haze. I continued down, looking for him.'

Seeing no sign of his element leader, Squire levelled off and searched the sky above for the rest of the squadron. They, too, were nowhere to be seen. Feeling very alone, he pulled his Spitfire round in a tight orbit to check for possible enemy fighters in the vicinity. Seeing none, and realizing he could do little by himself, he decided to get out of the area as quickly as possible. He pushed his throttle 'through the gate' for maximum emergency power and headed north.

'I had not got far when suddenly I saw red tracers streaking past my starboard side. Then there was an awful series of bangs as rounds struck my plane. In front of me the instruments in the blind flying panel disintegrated, and the wind came whistling through holes in my cockpit canopy.

'I looked around for my assailant but still I couldn't see where the attack was coming from. So I rolled the Spitfire on its back and pulled the stick hard into my stomach. The plane responded, there was no loss of control, but in my panic I pulled too hard and blacked out. I eased off on the stick and as the "g" came off I was able to see again. Then I realised I was going down almost vertically into the haze – and with no altimeter to warn me how much height I had left!'

Again Squire pulled out, again he looked around for his attacker and again he saw nothing. His engine had obviously been hit, and was running very rough with a lot of vibration.

'Again I turned back towards England, again tracers came past and again my Spitfire took hits. I did an aileron turn to shake off the attack, but although I searched the sky around I still could not see who was shooting at me. It was the classic case of a novice fighter failing to see what was happening around him.'

To make matters worse, the Spitfire's engine began to lose power. Squire made yet another turn to search the sky around,

and at last he caught sight of his enemy: eight Bf109s, four behind on his left and four on his right:

'The Messerschmitts had me cornered. I turned out to sea and one of them fired a deliberate burst of tracer past my nose. Now I was convinced I was not going to get back to England, and made up my mind to crash land wherever I could.'

The Spitfire continued its descent toward the port of Calais. From 500ft Squire could see the long strip of sandy beach to the east of the town, and decided on a suitable piece of flat sand on which to set down his crippled fighter. His main flying instruments shot away, he had to fly 'by the seat of his pants'. He pulled down his goggles, slid back the canopy and braced himself for the crash landing. As he neared the ground he throttled back, at which the engine stopped altogether.

'I saw what looked like an area of fairly flat sand inland, and aimed for that. But on rounding out I saw to my horror that what had looked like an area of flat sand was in fact a series of sand dunes. As I neared the first I eased back on the stick and just clipped the top; that killed a lot of my speed. Then there was a noise like a lot of tin trays being bashed together as the Spitfire slid down the side of the dune into a patch of marshy ground. As the plane slithered to a halt foul black slime came squirting up into the cockpit, past my feet and over me.'

Squire threw off his seat and parachute straps and clambered out of the cockpit, stepping off the wing into ankle-deep slime. To one side he could see figures running in his direction and someone fired a shot over his head. The young pilot crouched behind the tail of his plane and awaited to see what happened next:

'Suddenly several German soldiers arrived on the scene brandishing revolvers. I put my hands up initially but lowered them soon afterwards on my own account without anyone saying anything – it was pretty obvious I was not going anywhere!'

The men, from an army artillery unit located nearby, took their captive to a bunker a few hundred yards away. There Squire asked for 'Wasser', one of the few German words he knew, and someone brought a bowl of water, soap and a towel so he could clean the slime off his face and from the front of his uniform. Shortly afterwards a couple of Luftwaffe men arrived by car to collect him, one an Unteroffizier who spoke perfect English. They took the prisoner to the Officers' Mess at the fighter airfield at Calais-Marck, four miles from the scene of the crash.

The escorts ushered Squire into the ante-room, where several officers were gathered. He was offered a chair, given a glass of schnapps and introduced to the pilot of the Messerschmitt Bf109 that had shot him down: Hpt Herbert Ihlefeld, the commander of *I Gruppe* of *Lehrgeschwader 2* based at the airfield. A holder of

This page:
Squire and his captors inspect the remains of his slime-bespattered Spitfire near Calais. Accompanying him is Hauptmann Herbert Ihlefeld, the commander of *Ist Gruppe Lehrgeschwader 2,* who had shot him down a couple of hours earlier. *Djoud*

the coveted Ritterkreuz, Ihlefeld had notched up 25 victories by the end of the Battle of Britain. So this was the hardened professional whose skilful flying in combat had made Squire look a complete amateur!

'Ihlefeld did not speak English, but most of the other officers did and one translated for him. He said he was very pleased he had been able to shoot down my plane without causing any serious injury to me. Then he nodded to the table and asked if I had expected such treatment. I said I had, because if we in the RAF had the opportunity we would do the same. Everybody smiled and one of the Germans commented "Ah, we are all airman here . . .".

'After some more small-talk the intelligence officer quietly asked my squadron number. But when I refused to give it he shrugged his shoulders, grinned and said "Of course you don't tell me – you are a soldier, ja?". That was the end of the matter, nobody attempted to ask military questions after that. I thought they might try to ply me with booze to get me to talk, but they didn't. Everyone was very correct and friendly.'

Someone asked the prisoner if he was hungry, and when he said he was a steward brought a platter of garlic sausage sandwiches, and coffee. After he had eaten, Squire was asked if he had been hurt. During the crash landing his left hand had taken a nasty knock and it was starting to feel tender. The British pilot mentioned this, and was immediately driven back to Calais. There he received a full examination from a Luftwaffe doctor, who said the injury was not serious and would heal by itself (it later did).

From the surgery Squire was driven to one of the dispersal points at Calais-Marck, and was escorted up to a Bf109 and allowed to look round the outside. Then his captors said they would take him for a final look at the Spitfire. Having had time to collect his thoughts after the traumatic experience earlier in the day, the British pilot realised he had omitted to carry out one important duty. The only really sensitive item of equipment in the Spitfire was the Identification Friend or Foe set with its secret code settings. The equipment had a small destructor charge, which would fire if two plungers in the cockpit were pressed simultaneously. Now Squire's spirits rose: if only he could lean into the cockpit and set off the destructor . . .

Squire arrived at his plane to find it swarming with Germans, including Ihlefeld and several of the officers he had met at the airfield. Technicians had already removed several items of equipment, including the all-important IFF set.

'I was very put out by that; it spoilt the visit for me. People were taking photos, one of which showed my look of dejection on discovering I had handed a secret bit of equipment to the enemy.'

From the crash site Squire was driven back to Calais-Marck, where soon after his arrival he heard an animated discussion begin in German. Officers had arrived there from a nearby flak unit, claiming that it was they who had shot down the Spitfire. A few words from the captive settled the matter in Ihlefeld's favour.

Following more drinks, an Opel staff car arrived to collect the prisoner. After friendly handshakes all round and fare-wells, Howard Squire set out to begin a captivity that would last more than four years. It had been, in every respect, a day to remember.

Herbert Ihlefeld continued to build up his score, and would end the war an oberst-leutnant credited with 140 victories. In July 1984, after being contacted by Winston Ramsey the editor of *After the Battle* magazine, the German fighter ace returned to Calais to resume his acquaintance with the Spitfire pilot he had shot down 43 years earlier. It was a fitting end to the story of chivalrous treatment afforded by an airman to a vanquished foe.

Right:
Howard Squire, left, and Herbert Ihlefeld pictured together at the same spot in 1984.
Winston Ramsey

10 Spitfire Night Fighters

In August 1941 Sgt Peter Durnford joined No 111 Squadron at North Weald flying Spitfire Vs, having come straight from training. He quickly became operational and took part in several convoy patrols and fighter sweeps over occupied Europe. At the beginning of November the squadron moved to Debden and, with the similarly equipped No 65 Squadron, began night flying training sorties.

When night flying was taking place at Debden, the grass runway was marked on one side by a line of Glim lamps (battery powered portable lights). Getting airborne at night in a Spitfire was simple enough, Durnford recalled, provided the pilot learned to ignore certain distractions:

'You had to take off with the hood open, or as you went past the Glim lights their light reflected off the canopy and seemed to flash all over the place. But when you opened the throttle with the hood open a stream of exhaust sparks would swirl into the cockpit during take-off (it also happened if you took off by day with the canopy open, but then you never noticed them!). Initially we had a lot of glare from the circular exhaust stubs, too. The only thing to do was get airborne quickly, then throttle back and close the canopy. It was one of the things you had to get used to.'

The only item of self-contained navigation equipment carried by the Spitfire was the compass. To return to Debden at the end of the sortie, pilots had to rely on VHF radio bearings and homings from base.

'Once near the airfield you could locate the Chance light, flashing the code of the day. Knowing where it was placed (it was in a different position each night), you could position yourself for a curved approach and pick up the glide path indicator and the Glim lamps during the last stage of the descent.

'In the Spitfire a long straight-in engine-on approach was difficult at night, because the engine cowling blocked the view ahead and you couldn't see the runway lights. You had to make a curved approach to keep the runway in sight.'

In December, No 111 Squadron returned to North Weald for a few days, then on 23 December the unit received orders to go back to Debden. On arrival the unit's pilots learned that, with No 65 Squadron, they were now to operate in the night-fighter role. The concern was that the Luftwaffe might resume large-scale night attacks on Britain at any time, and the two squadrons were to provide a high speed night interception capability.

Once the two squadrons were established in the new role, their Spitfires were repainted in matt black overall. National markings and squadron codes were retained on the fuselage and fin, but those above and below the wings were painted over. The ground crews fitted 'fishtail' exhausts in place of the previous circular exhausts, to reduce exhaust glare during night flying. On Christmas Eve 1941 Peter Durnford flew a 1hr 10min night sector reconnaissance patrol over East Anglia. From then on the two squadrons flew patrols on nearly every evening the weather allowed.

If German bombers resumed night attacks, the two Spitfire squadrons were to employ the 'Smack' interception procedure working in conjunction with radar-laid searchlights. When enemy aircraft were detected approaching the coast, the sector controller was to order the fighters to scramble. The Spitfires were to take off individually and climb to a pre-briefed altitude, each making for its patrol area marked by a single vertical searchlight beam. On arrival the Spitfire was to orbit near the beam and wait. When an enemy aircraft neared the area the searchlight beam would waver for a short time, then depress to 20° pointing in the direction in which the fighter was to head.

'We would fly along the beam until another searchlight came on, pointing up vertically. Then it would waggle and point in the next direction we were to go. When we got close to the intruder we were to get a radio call "Cone!", and several searchlights would switch on and cone the target with their beams. Once we had the target in sight we were to engage it.'

Below:
Sgt Peter Durnford of No 111 Squadron pictured in the cockpit of his Spitfire.
Durnford

No III SQUADRON

This page:
Peter Durnford's Spitfire JU-H pictured at Debden, December 1941. The aircraft was painted matt-black overall, and wore no serial number and no roundels above or below the wings. The aircraft carried normal fuselage roundels, and toned-down identification letters. *Durnford*

Although the two Spitfire squadrons regularly practised the 'Smack' procedures, for some reason they were not allowed to test them against friendly aircraft; the first time the pilots flew the full procedure would be against the enemy. In the event the Spitfires were never put to the test, however, for the expected enemy attacks failed to materialise. The final part of December 1941, January and the first 11 days of February 1942, proved particularly quiet over Britain and Spitfire pilots never got so much as a glimpse of an enemy plane at night. The night operations continued until 12 February, when there was excitement from a quite different quarter. The battle cruisers *Scharnhorst* and *Gneisenau* and the cruiser *Prinz Eugen*, escorted by several smaller warships and almost every German fighter in the area, were forcing a passage through the English Channel on their way back to Germany.

'We had been on readiness during the night, sleeping in the dispersal hut. There was some local flying in the morning, then we knocked off. Suddenly we were called back to readiness. The Wing Commander Flying dashed into the briefing room and said "The German fleet is coming through the Channel, follow me!".

'He took off and we followed. We were supposed to rendezvous with the Spitfire squadrons from North Weald, but the weather was terrible and we missed them. We went out over the sea, and the next thing I knew we had run into a whole lot of 109s. There was a terrific low level scrap and our squadron was split up. I fired on an Me109 and saw strikes around the cockpit, it rolled on its back and went down. Due to the very low height, 100ft or so, it must

Peter Durnford's dog, Duffy, pictured on the wing of one of the black Spitfires. Note the baffles to shield the pilot's eyes from the exhaust glare, and the fish-tail exhaust stubs. *Durnford*

Left:
Spitfire JU-E flown by the squadron commander, Sqn Ldr Brotchie, showing the small fuselage roundels carried by the unit's aircraft from February 1942. *Durnford*

have gone in (I was later awarded a "Probable").

'Then I passed over some ships which threw a lot of flak at me and my No 2. We got separated and in the end I decided to go home, I was getting short of fuel. Visibility was poor and I had a job finding somewhere to land. In the end I put down at North Weald and just as I landed the prop stopped. I had run out of fuel, after 2hr 10min airborne.'

That would prove to be Peter Durnford's sole encounter with the enemy while flying a black Spitfire. Following the passage of the German ships the two squadrons ceased night operations, and the following month their Spitfires were repainted in normal day-fighter colours. Summing up the Spitfire night fighter operations, he commented:

'It has been said the Spitfire was not suitable for night flying. Personally, I think the suitability of the aircraft depended on the suitability of the pilot. I enjoyed night flying and I never had any problems. I was fairly confident we could have intercepted enemy planes using the "Smack" procedure. But some pilots had a twitch about flying at night, for them everything was wrong and they weren't going to find a thing. As they said "Only birds and fools fly, and birds don't fly at night".'

11 A Fair Day's Work

In July 1941 No 1 Photographic Unit was a squadron-sized unit with its main base at Benson near Oxford, and a detached flight at St Eval in Cornwall. Listed below are the missions flown on one day that month, the 17th, by the unit's Spitfires. Beside the serial number of each aircraft is the letter denoting the version of reconnaissance Spitfire. Unless otherwise stated, all missions were flown at high altitude.

Below:
Sorties flown by No 1 PRU On 17 July 1941.

Serial/Version	Take-off	Time Airborne	Targets
X4494/F	0700	1.30	Brest (from St Eval)
X4491/F	0855	4.20	Kiel-Brunsbuttel-Cuxhaven
X4384/F	0915	2.25	Brest. Took off from Benson, landed at St Eval
R6900/C	0930	3.05	Airfields: Aachen, Coblenz, Düsseldorf
X4672/G	0930	2.10	Airfields in Abbeville-Amiens area, low altitude
X4497/C	0950	3.55	Kastrup-Copenhagen
X4333-C	0950	3.05	Valenciennes-Hazebrook-Vimy-Arras
X4334/C	0950	3.00	Airfields in SE Belgium
P9550/C	0957	4.03	Hamburg-Bremen-Emden-Delfzijl
X4492/F	0958	3.12	Amsterdam-Ijmuiden

Serial/Version	Take-off	Time Airborne	Targets
X4491/F	1400	4.45	Montlucon-Limoges
X4672/G	1400	2.00	Cap Barfleur-Dieppe, low altitude
R6900/C	1405	2.20	Flushing, airfields in Ghent-Bruges area
X4334/C	1350	2.50	Airfields E of Paris
X4492/F	1525	2.50	Airfields Orleans-Etaples area
P9550/C	1630	2.15	Caen-Falaise area
X4384/F	1815	1.30	Guernsey-St Malo-Rennes-Brest (from St Eval)
R7059/G	1830	2.00	Brest, low altitude (from St Eval)
P9550/C	1915	1.15	Cherbourg
X4384/F	2020	1.15	Brest (from St Eval)

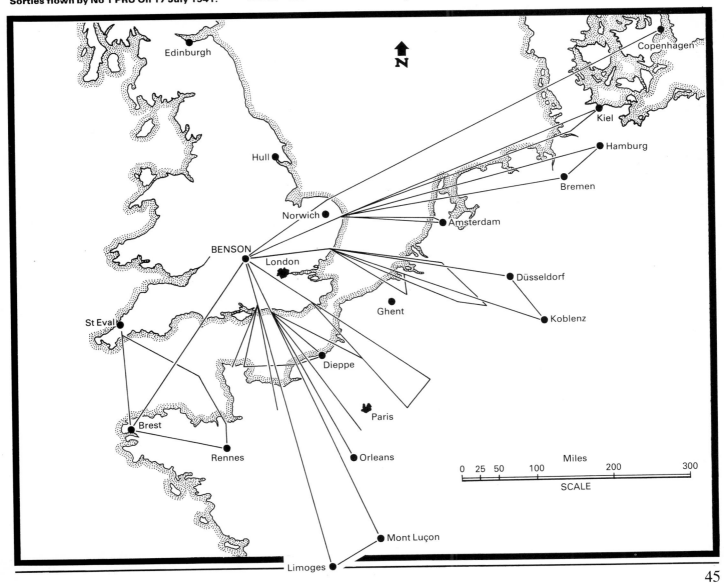

During the day the unit's 11 serviceable Spitfires flew 20 sorties. All aircraft returned safely. Three versions of reconnaissance Spitfire were flown by the unit: the PR IC (nine sorties flown), the PR IF (eight) and the PR IG (three sorties flown).

The PR IC had the guns and radio removed, and carried two vertical cameras in a blister under the starboard wing, a 30gal blister fuel tank under the port wing and a 29gal extra fuel tank in the rear fuselage (total fuel tankage 144gal).

The PR IF had the guns and radio removed and carried two vertical cameras in the rear fuselage, a 30gal blister tank under each wing and a 29gal tank in the rear fuselage (total fuel tankage 174gal).

The PR IG version was used for short range low altitude 'dicing' missions. It retained the fighter's eight-gun armament but the radio was removed. This version carried two vertical and one oblique cameras, and a 29gal extra fuel tank in the rear fuselage (total fuel tankage 114gal).

The two longest sorties, to Kiel in the morning and to Limoges in the afternoon, were both flown by PR IF serial X4491. This aircraft spent a total of 9hr 5min airborne that day, a remarkable figure.

The above section shows the wealth of intelligence on enemy dispositions brought in on a single day by just one squadron-sized reconnaissance unit.

This picture:
Spitfire PR IF, serial X4384, pictured at St Eval. This aircraft flew three sorties to photograph Brest on 17 July 1941.

Right and below:
Pilots of No 1 PRU: David Salwey, pictured (*below left*) later in the war after promotion to Sqn Ldr; Flg Off Don Steventon (*right*); Flg Off Alistair Taylor (*below right*).

12 No 11 Group Tactical Memorandum No 14

This tactical paper, issued at the beginning of 1942, outlined the tactics to be employed by fighter units during offensive and bomber escort operations over Northern Europe. Incorporating the lessons of more than 18 months' aerial fighting, the paper was an altogether more realistic treatise on the subject than the paper issued in the early summer of 1940 reproduced at Chapter 6.

1 The object of this Memorandum is to bring up to date and consolidate in one document the tactical instructions on offensive operations which have been written during 1941 as a result of experience gained over the Channel and Northern France. It is a verbatim reproduction of 11 Group's Tactical Memorandum No 14 (which cancels that Group's earlier Tactical Memos Nos 1 to 12). It also supersedes the information in Air Fighting Committee Paper No 115 (Fighter Escort Tactics), all copies of which should be annotated accordingly.

2 Aim of Offensive Operations by Our Fighters Over Enemy Occupied Territory
The aims of these offensive operations are:

(i) To destroy enemy aircraft
(ii) To force the enemy to increase his fighter strength in the West at the expense of other vital fronts
(iii) To dislocate transport and industry
(iv) To obtain moral superiority in our fighting
(v) To build up and maintain a high standard of fighting efficiency in our squadrons.

3 Conditions Under Which Offensive Fighter Operations are Carried Out
Operations by single-seater fighters over enemy occupied territory suffer from two handicaps:
(i) That sooner or later the fighters must turn for home, and they then become more vulnerable to attack by enemy fighters, and
(ii) damage to aircraft which — over our own territory — would only cause a forced landing or a parachute descent, is liable to lead to the loss of both pilot and aircraft.
It is consequently essential that squadrons taking part in these preparations should be highly trained both in air fighting and in giving mutual support, and such operations should be carefully designed to offer the best prospects of success (including diversions in time and height) and that pilots should be carefully briefed as to their roles.

A pilot of No 313 (Czech) Squadron runs to his Spitfire.

4 Our fighter squadrons in the air are now organised on the basis of the 'pair' of aircraft as the smallest formation. Two pairs work as a 'four' and three fours make a squadron. Each squadron on a large operation is, moreover, given its role as part of a Wing, and each Wing has a specified part to play. A nice balance must be kept between compactness and flexibility. Aircraft must be in mutual support while still being free to manoeuvre and fight.

A high standard has been reached in carrying out these operations in 1941 for, despite the inherent handicap of an offensive by fighters, and despite the fact that the Germans — as always — try to evade action unless in a superior position and even then usually confine such action to the diving tactics for which the Me109F is well suited, (rather than the 'dogfights' which suit the Hurricane and Spitfire), we have on 96 'Circuses' destroyed 574 enemy aircraft, probably destroyed 257 and damaged 309 for the loss of 283 fighter pilots [these claims were considerably in excess of the actual German losses — author]. During these operations, some 759 bombers have been escorted and only 16 have been lost, 11 by flak, three by enemy fighter action and two by unknown causes.

5 Types of Offensive Operations
For brevity of description, offensive operations have been given the following code names:

CIRCUS
An attack by bombers, escorted by fighters in which the object of the attack is primarily to bring the enemy fighters to action.

RAMROD
An attack by bombers (or fighter/bombers) escorted by fighters in which the destruction of the target is the primary object.

RODEO
A fighter sweep without bombers.

ROADSTEAD
An attack on enemy shipping by bombers (or fighter/bombers) escorted by fighters.

RHUBARB
A small scale attack by fighters using cloud cover and surprise, the objectives being enemy aircraft in the air, and worthwhile targets on the ground or sea.

6 Method of Execution
The following brief description of the manner in which a *CIRCUS* is carried out is also applicable to *RAMRODS*, *ROADSTEADS* and *RODEOS*, with certain modifications which are referred to later. *RHUBARBS* are a different class of operation, and their method of execution is later referred to separately.

Orders for the operation are issued by Form D, or if time is short, by telephone on the operational lines, and detail the forces to be employed, the rendezvous, the target and bombing heights, the role of the forces, the route and timings at various points, the direction of turn by the bombers over the target and special signal arrangements.

7 The bombers should arrive at the rendezvous — which should be a fairly prominent landmark — a few minutes before zero hour, in order to assist the fighters in joining up with them without wasting the fighters' petrol. Both bombers and fighters should as soon as possible gain height and approach the rendezvous in manner best calculated to minimise the time of warning given by the enemy RDF. The bombers should leave the rendezvous at zero hour and not before, having satisfied themselves that their escort and other supporting fighters have arrived. W/T silence will be maintained, except in emergency, until the enemy coast is reached. Bombers should fly in a 'box' as compact as possible, avoiding straggling or wasting time over enemy territory, and on reaching the English coast on return should steer a course inland and not remain near the coast any longer than necessary.

8 Roles of the Fighters
(i) ESCORT WING
  (a) The role of this Wing is to protect the bombers from interference by enemy fighters. This Wing must remain with the bombers as far as possible, and during the whole of the penetration and withdrawal, they must not be drawn off.
  (b) The Wing consists normally of three or four squadrons. Originally, it consisted of three squadrons, but it was found necessary to provide an additional squadron to protect the bombers from enemy fighter attacks from below. Consequently, one of the escort squadrons was detailed to this role. The remaining two or three squadrons of the Escort Wing provide close protection against attacks from above.

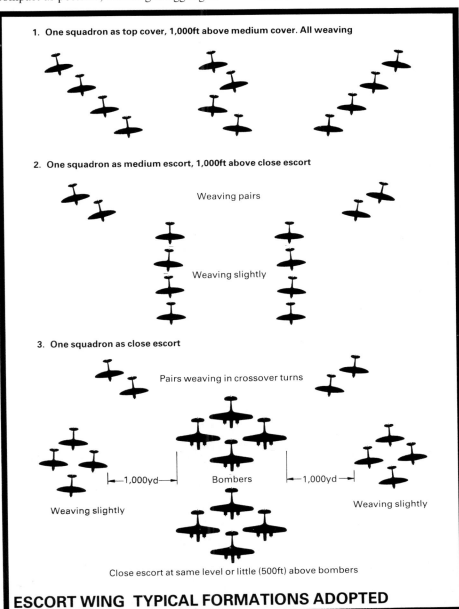

1. One squadron as top cover, 1,000ft above medium cover. All weaving

2. One squadron as medium escort, 1,000ft above close escort

Weaving pairs

Weaving slightly

3. One squadron as close escort

Pairs weaving in crossover turns

|←1,000yd→| Bombers |←1,000yd→|

Weaving slightly

Weaving slightly

Close escort at same level or little (500ft) above bombers

ESCORT WING TYPICAL FORMATIONS ADOPTED

(c) The role of the squadron providing the close escort is to stay to protect the bombers under all circumstances. They are there in a purely defensive role, and must not be led away into a fight.

(d) The second squadron is free to engage and fight any enemy fighters attacking our bombers.

(e) The third and top squadron acts as a top cover for the Escort Wing, and should remain in position as far as possible.

(f) The fourth squadron in the Escort Wing acts as underneath cover for the bombers, as it has been found that enemy fighters sometimes attempt to get at our bombers by diving down behind, and coming up from below. This squadron normally flies 1,000ft below bomber height, and in the same formation as the first squadron of the close Escort Wing. This fourth squadron should open to the flanks in flak areas, but should remain under the umbrella cover above.

(g) All squadrons in the Escort Wing weave continuously.

(h) The height interval between each squadron in the Escort Wing is 1,000-1,500ft.

(ii) ESCORT COVER WING

(a) The role of this Wing is to protect the bombers and the Escort Wing.

(b) The bottom squadron of this Wing is usually about 1,000ft above the top squadron of the close escort, the second squadron being 1,000ft above the bottom squadron and the third squadron 2,000ft above the middle squadron. The Wing should be able to prevent enemy fighters from positioning themselves for a favourable attack on the Escort Wing and bombers.

(c) This Wing normally consists of three squadrons. It has a greater freedom of action than the Escort Wing and usually flies in a more open formation.

(d) This Wing makes the same rendezvous with the bomber formation and flies the same course out and home as the bombers and Escort Wing.

(e) One essential rule for this Wing is that it should be up sun of the main formation, and squadrons in the Wing should be stepped up sun of each other.

(f) As long as at least one squadron of the Wing remains as top cover, the lower squadrons are free to engage and fight the enemy.

(iii) HIGH COVER

(a) The role of this Wing is to protect the Escort Cover Wing. It flies in a more open formation and has greater freedom of action than the other two Wings.

(b) This Wing consists normally of three squadrons. The formations vary and are left to the discretion of the Wing and the squadron leaders. The three squad-

rons are stepped up from the Escort Cover at 1,000, 2,000, 4,000-5,000ft intervals.

(c) This Wing should be up sun of the Escort Cover Wing and squadrons in the Wing are stepped up sun of each other. All the squadrons weave and the two lower squadrons are free to engage the enemy as long as the highest squadron remains as top cover.

(iv) TARGET SUPPORT WINGS

(a) The role of these Wings is to achieve air superiority on the route to the target and over the target area itself, prior to the arrival of the bombers. As soon as the Wings arrive over the target they split into sections of four and cover the whole area at varying heights above the bombers.

(b) One Wing usually approaches on approximately the same line as the bombers, but overtaking them on the way to the target. This Wing must deal with any opposition met with on the way to the target.

(c) Other Wings take the most suitable route as selected for the operation, and remain over the target until after the bombing and then cover the withdrawal of the bombers and Escort Wing.

(d) It might be thought that the advantage of surprise would be lost by indicating our selected targets in this way. This is not so, however, because as soon as the enemy RDF system indicates an approaching raid, enemy fighter patrols are put up in the vicinity of all the important targets.

(v) THE FORWARD SUPPORT WING

(a) The role of this Wing is to cover the withdrawal of the bombers and the escorting fighters. The Wing is positioned on the withdrawal route of the bombers either on, or a few miles inside the French coast. They should be at high or medium altitude according to the expected height of the enemy. The Forward Support Wing will take up its position shortly before the bombers are due to cross its patrol line on their

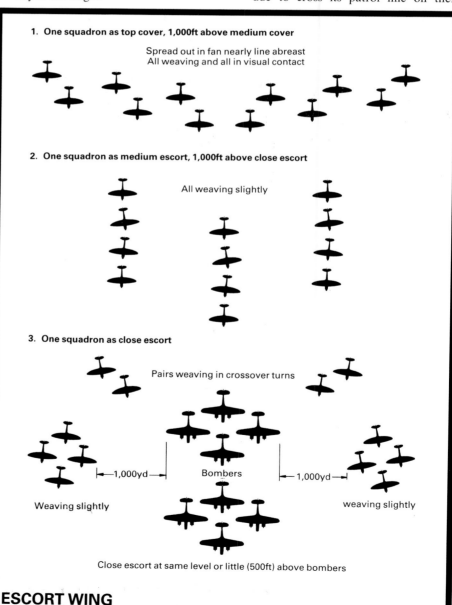

1. One squadron as top cover, 1,000ft above medium cover

Spread out in fan nearly line abreast
All weaving and all in visual contact

2. One squadron as medium escort, 1,000ft above close escort

All weaving slightly

3. One squadron as close escort

Pairs weaving in crossover turns

1,000yd — Bombers — 1,000yd

Weaving slightly — weaving slightly

Close escort at same level or little (500ft) above bombers

ESCORT WING

return. As this Wing will have fuller petrol tanks than the Wings which have been the whole way to the target, it will be in a position to stay and fight while the main force returns.

(b) This Wing should remain in its patrol area for some minutes after the withdrawal of the bombers and their escort in order to prevent the enemy following the main formation back to the English coast.

(vi) THE REAR SUPPORT WING

(a) The role of this Wing which may consist of only two squadrons is to act as a reserve in position about half-way across the Channel at medium altitude and is capable of being directed quickly to reinforce any of our forces which are in trouble on their return.

(b) This Wing takes off in time to be in position a few minutes before the main force approaches the French coast on its return journey.

(c) On some occasions, this Wing may be used to patrol an area about 10 miles off the English coast from 1,000-10,000ft. The reason for this positioning is that on many occasions enemy aircraft have crossed the Channel from the French coast very low and have pulled up to a medium height near the English coast. They have then dived for France, shooting down any of our stragglers or damaged aircraft returning at low altitude.

9 The above detail gives the task of each Wing, but it is not necessary for all those Wings to be employed in every *CIRCUS*. Much depends on the position of the target and the estimated strength of enemy opposition. Throughout the summer, the tactical situation has been changing constantly and at certain times it was only necessary to have one Target Support Wing. The enemy later increased his opposition and made it necessary for the provision of a second Wing with the same role.

Similarly, one can dispense with a Forward Support Wing for targets close to the French coast. When particularly strong opposition is expected, very successful operations have been carried out by staging one *Circus* some minutes before another. The first one will not penetrate deeply and its object will be to draw up as many enemy fighters as possible. Then when the aircraft are going down to land, the second main penetration will take place.

10 Formations and Fighting Tactics Used by Our Fighters

In paragraph 4 above, a few general remarks were included on the manner in which our fighter formations are organised; and at Appendices 'A' and 'B' attached, are diagrams showing different formations used by the Escort Wing. Appendix 'C' shows two methods of turning adopted by a squadron to meet attacks.

11 The Germans like to make a surprise pecking attack and then get away as quickly as possible. Each squadron, therefore, needs a well-though-out and practical plan of action to meet this form of attack. Two cardinal principles may be laid down:

(i) Always turn to the attack.

(ii) Try to maintain height and tactical cohesion. Scattering is no good. To fulfil both of these conditions, a flexible and manoeuvrable formation is necessary, and either the whole formation can turn, or Flights or pairs can turn outwards and form circles at the same height. This caters for attack or quick re-forming.

Surprise by the enemy must also be avoided. This can best be achieved by weavers — placed about 550ft above and below the formation and just ahead of it, or by the weaving of the whole formation or of selected pairs. Many formations can be adopted, each probably equally good, but each form adopted must be flexible and manoeuvrable without being rigid. If weavers are employed, these should be changed at frequent intervals.

It is also essential to have a plan laid down for the detachment of the formation of a suitable attacking force according to the target presented. At least one third of the force should, however, remain above as an 'umbrella' but the force sent down must be capable of fighting its own way out. Where the role of the Wing concerned is to seek out and destroy the enemy, all leaders must be alert for these detachments.

East aircraft of a pair should be about 50yd apart, and each pair about 100yd apart. Close to our own territory these distances can be opened out somewhat as this affords greater flexibility for attack.

12 The following points have also been found of value in offensive operations:

(i) Never fly immediately below a cloud level, leave a sighting gap of at least 2,000ft — or else put another force just above the cloud. Similarly it is unwise to fly immediately above a cloud layer, owing to the clear silhouette given.

(ii) Always try to withdraw across sun

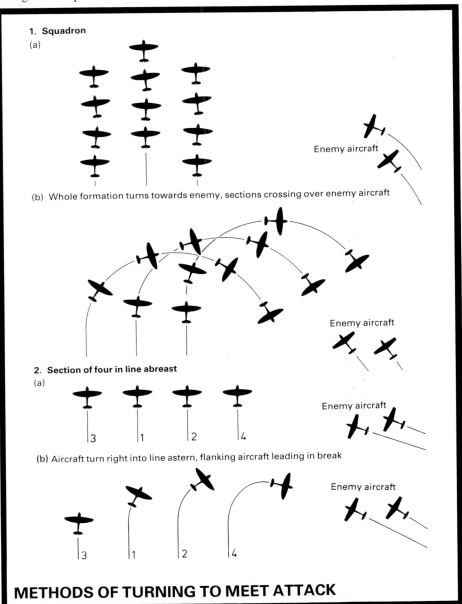

1. Squadron
(a)

Enemy aircraft

(b) Whole formation turns towards enemy, sections crossing over enemy aircraft

Enemy aircraft

2. Section of four in line abreast
(a)

3 1 2 4

(b) Aircraft turn right into line astern, flanking aircraft leading in break

Enemy aircraft

3 1 2 4

Enemy aircraft

METHODS OF TURNING TO MEET ATTACK

— unfortunately we cannot often withdraw up-sun.

(iii) Plessey devices (remote controlled flare dispensers) are not to be used for recognition by day fighters, but only to indicate distress, when red lights will be fired.

(iv) Many German pilots dive away at the first opportunity when engaged, and are at an advantage in so doing as their engines are not affected by negative 'g', moreover the Me109 has a good initial acceleration. Under such circumstances, a good following manoeuvre is to roll down after the enemy.

13 Types of Offensive Operations Other Than 'Circuses'

In paragraph 4, reference was made to five types of operations, but only the method of execution of a *CIRCUS* has been detailed above.

RAMROD is identical to a *CIRCUS* in execution, except that the destruction of enemy aircraft is incidental and is not the main object of the operation. More fighter-bombers are used instead of bombers, the number accompanying fighters can be reduced.

Above:
A couple of Mk IIas of No 602 Squadron pictured at Heathfield adjacent to Prestwick, in April 1941. The aircraft in the foreground LO-L, was P8047, and not P3047 as it appears at first sight. *Cameron*

RODEO is also similar though there are no bombers and consequently there is no Escort Wing. Target Support Wings are not necessary, and the object is to destroy enemy aircraft. A good plan of execution — which must not be used too often — is to sweep a Wing or Wings through — say 20 miles in at 15,000ft — and follow it 10min later by another force with less penetration and greater height.

ROADSTEAD is usually composed of eight anti-flak Hurricanes, four Hurricane bombers and two Spitfire squadrons. The rendezvous is carried out below 500ft to cheat the enemy RDF [radar] and the whole force is led by the anti-flak aircraft; go out at sea level. When the target is

sighted, the anti-flak Hurricanes (both cannon and 12-gun types) pull up to about 2,000ft and then dive on the flak ships. The Hurricane bombers pull up with them and go down on their tails to get the benefit of the anti-flak fire, and pull their bombs off as low as possible (11sec delay). Meanwhile the two Spitfire squadrons have pulled up to 3,000ft and 5,000ft. As many flak ships as possible should be attacked out of the sun. There should only be the shortest practicable delay between the anti-flak attack and the bombing.

RHUBARB as described, take advantage of cloud cover — which should be adequate for concealment and should have a base of at least 1,500ft for safety in breaking cloud. If cloud is not satisfactory, the aircraft which are not more than one pair, should return immediately. *RHUBARB* aircraft should be detailed a route and time, and given an area in which to break cloud. Their first objective is enemy aircraft in the air, but the area will also contain alternative ground objectives, concerning which pilots must be carefully briefed, but they should not take unnecessary risks to find the ground target if it is not at once located.

13 First Spitfires to Malta

Until the spring of 1942, no Spitfire fighter squadron had been based outside Great Britain. Early in that year, however, the air situation in Malta reached a critical stage. The Hurricanes defending the island were outclassed by the new F version of the Messerschmitt Bf109, and there was a serious risk that the latter might establish air superiority over that beleaguered island.

Malta's strategic importance in the Mediterranean stemmed from its use as a base for the bombers and torpedo-bombers which took a steady toll of the ships transporting supplies and reinforcements for the German and Italian armies in North Africa. Whenever the latter were about to launch a new offensive in the Western Desert, there was usually a series of heavy air attacks on Malta to neutralise its aerial strike forces. At the end of 1941 the combined German and Italian High Command decided to lance the Maltese abscess: the island was to be seized in a combined airborne and seaborne assault.

As a preliminary to invasion, early in 1942 the Luftwaffe began concentrating units at airfields in Sicily and the number of aircraft on the island increased from about 200 to more than 400. About half of the total were bombers, Junkers Ju87s and Ju88s, and more than 100 of the new Bf109Fs were deployed to support their attacks. The bombardment of Malta opened in January and rapidly gained in momentum.

The continued survival of Malta would depend to a large extent on its fighter defences. But when fighters were lost, and many were during the hard-fought air battles, their replacement required considerable effort. The island lay 1,380 statute miles to the east of Gibraltar, beyond the maximum ferry range of any existing British single-engined fighter. Moreover the strength of the enemy air forces in Sicily ruled out the delivery of fighters to the island by freighter: any attempt to do so would almost certainly have resulted in a full scale battle, with heavy losses and little prospect of success.

At that time Hurricanes for the island were transported by aircraft carrier to a launching point off the coast of Algeria, where they took off and flew the rest of the way to Malta. The distance, 660 miles by the shortest practical route, was about as great as that from London to Prague and for the flight the planes were fitted with two 44gal underwing tanks. Despite the large naval effort necessary for each delivery operation, this was the only practicable method. Several such operations were mounted and by the end of 1941 more than 300 Hurricanes had reached the island in this way.

Now there was a clear requirement for Spitfires to be sent to Malta, and they too were to be taken half way by aircraft carrier. To enable these aircraft to cover the rest of the distance, at the highest priority a new 90gal jettisonable slipper tank was developed and a small batch was manufactured. These Spitfires were also the first production machines fitted with tropical filters for the carburettor air intake, necessary to prevent dust and sand getting into the engine and causing excessive wear.

At the beginning of February 1942 the process of delivering the first contingent of Spitfires to Malta, codenamed Operation 'Spotter', entered its final stage. Under conditions of great secrecy, 16 crated fighters were loaded on the freighter *Cape Hawk* berthed at Liverpool. The ship also carried 16 pilots for No 249 Squadron and about 100 groundcrew, with Wg Cdr Maclean in charge of the entire detachment.

Cape Hawk set sail from Liverpool on the afternoon of 9 February as part of an escorted convoy. Except for the commander and the senior engineering officer, the members of the RAF contingent were ignorant of their intended destination. Everyone had been issued with tropical kit and fully 'jabbed up', however, so it was clear they were bound for somewhere warm. LAC George Revell, one of those on the freighter, later recalled:

'The news was put up as a daily bulletin, and there was consternation that the German warships *Scharnhorst*, *Gneisenau* and *Prinz Eugen* had broken out of Brest. Also Singapore had fallen, so we wouldn't be going there!'

The most popular rumour among the 'erks' was that they were on their way to the USA, for a course of instruction on the maintenance of American aircraft and engines.

Cpl Ray Honeybone, another member of the detachment, had previously worked on Spitfires while serving as an engine fitter on No 501 Squadron at Ibsley. After 10 days at sea, he and a few other NCOs were summoned to go to see Sqn Ldr 'Shorty' Hughes, the detachment's senior engineering officer. After being sworn not to divulge what they were about to see, the men were led into the bowels of the ship:

'In one hold into which we passed were 16 large wooden cases, but we were told to break open some smaller cases at the far end. After the first two or three lids had been lifted off and the contents laid bare, there was enough evidence to kill once and for all the myth of "an aero engine course in the States". At that stage of the war a fitter's tool kit looked like the next fitter's tool kit, but the tools we unwrapped had a special look about them – a Supermariney sort of look – as if some poor rigger was expected to stick mainplanes to fuselages.

Below:
Ray Honeybone, left, and two other RAF fitters on HMS *Eagle*, March 1942. *Honeybone*

And the jacking equipment looked familiar – like the sort of stuff we had left in the Bessoneau hangar in Ibsley. It didn't need a super-spy to work out what the 16 large cases held! However, we feigned ignorance and built up a few wingtip, belly and tail trestles. After all, there was nowhere else to go that afternoon . . .'

The *Cape Hawk* arrived at Gibraltar on 21 February and entered the inner harbour where she tied up next to the aircraft carrier HMS *Eagle*. Work began immediately to offload the crates, and by the following day all 16 were lined up on the quayside beside the ship. There the boxes were to remain, however, for it was essential to keep the movement of the fighters a secret from the enemy as long as possible. It was known that German agents kept watch on the port from the Spanish town of Algeciras on the other side of the bay. And each day several hundred Spaniards came to work on Gibraltar, returning each evening before nightfall; it was believed that some of the workers were also being paid by the Germans to report anything of interest seen at the port.

To keep secret the existence of the batch of Spitfires on Gibraltar, the crates were not opened until after dark on the 22nd. Ray Honeybone described the start of the operation:

'As the end was unbolted from the first of the large cases, a Spitfire fuselage was revealed. The fuselage with the engine in position lay in the centre, with the mainplanes mounted on the side walls. The propeller was mounted on one side wall. The drill was to drag the fuselage out of its cradle, transfer it to a set of belly jacks, manoeuvre out each mainplane in turn, fit the main and rear spar bolts, then drop and lock down the undercarriage units. This gave us a mobile structure, to which the propeller was fitted prior to lifting the aircraft on board the carrier . . .'

George Revell takes up the story, and explains how the need for secrecy dominated every part of the operation:

'This activity was taking place at night, but with a generous amount of lighting as Gib

This page:
Due to the extreme secrecy afforded to Operation 'Spotter', it is believed no photographs were taken. These shots were from the second Spitfire delivery to the island, Operation 'Picket 1' on 21 March 1942, and show the aircraft taking off from HMS *Eagle* while HMS *Argus* in the background provides fighter cover for the operation. *IWM*

The largest deliveries of Spitfires to Malta
were the operations involving the USS *Wasp*

Left:
The deck of *Wasp* late on the afternoon of
19 April 1942, with long shadows on the deck
as the ships heads east. Ranged ready to take
off at first light the next morning are the
American carrier's Wildcats which will cover
the fly-off. In the background are Spitfires of
No 603 Squadron.

Below:
Spitfires taking off from Wasp on the morning
of the 20th. Once those parked at the rear of
the carrier had gone, those in the ship's
hangar were brought up one at a time and
sent off. Forty-seven spitfires took off from
the carrier that day; 46 reached Malta.

In May *Wasp* delivered a further batch of
Spitfires to Malta, this time in company with
HMS *Eagle*.

Right:
Wasp's hangar packed with Spitfires for this
operation.

Below right:
Wasp's flight deck on the morning of 9 May
with *Eagle* in the background, approaching
the flying-off point. During this operation 64
Spitfires were launched; 60 reached Malta.
USN

wasn't blacked out unless an "alert" was
sounded. However, to reduce the chances
of our "friends" across the bay seeing too
much, the lighting on the flight deck was
kept to a minimum, particularly when the
loads reached flight deck level.'

Also, as each Spitfire came on board, a
party of sailors at one end of the flight deck
would start the engine on one of *Eagle's*
Sea Hurricanes to serve as a diversion.
Once on deck, the Spitfire was wheeled
across the flight deck to the lift and taken
below.

The work went on throughout the hours
of darkness then, as Ray Honeybone

explained, as dawn approached the aircraft
crates on the quay were restored to make it
appear as if nothing had happened:

'To keep up the pretence of secrecy, each
empty case was re-assembled to make it
look as though nothing had been dis-
turbed. As first light appeared at 04.00hr,
we assembled our camp beds on the
hangar floor and crashed to sleep. In no
time at all it was 08.00hr and we learnt
that the 1st and 2nd Dog were not
Yorkshire terriers, and with only four
hours sleep it was a sharp breakfast, then
back to the hangar to carry on making the
"Spits" operational.'

The last four of the Spitfires were hoisted
on to *Eagle's* flight deck during the small
hours of the 25th. Now the work of
re-assembling the fighters went ahead at
top speed. The 'erks' were divided into
eight gangs, each comprising a corporal
and three men, and each gang was
allocated two Spitfires to work on. Several
members of the detachment had previously
worked at Maintenance Units and were
familiar with the repair and re-assembly of
Spitfires. Although these were brand new
aircraft some of the parts needed to be
changed. There were no spare parts so
Hughes decided to cannibalise one of the
fighters to provide spares for the rest.

Ray Honeybone described the work of re-assembling the Spitfires and getting them ready for flight:

'There were coolant joints to make, hydraulic and air systems to complete, controls to connect and adjust, all the myriad jobs which on a squadron you did occasionally, one at a time as rectification we now did all at once and in record time.

'We'd had a shock the first night when the first prop went on. De Havilland provided a special spanner for tightening the prop hub nut and the cylinder cover, and this tool hadn't come to light amongst the rest of the special equipment. From memory a drawing was made, dimensions determined, and with the co-operation of the Royal Engineers workshop we had a tool that did as good a job as the real thing. On the third night ashore the dock party opened the last but one aircraft crate and there found a DH prop-fitting kit.

'A feature new to all of us was the auxiliary fuel tank which held 90gal of 100 octane. These we were told were necessary to double the range of the Spitfire so that it could get to where it was going; basic thinking, but necessary. Under the fuselage and in line with the mainplanes was a three-point mounting, the centre one of which was retractable so that the tank could be jettisoned. There was also a device consisting of a spring-loaded mushroom valve in the cockpit floor which mated with a seating on the upper surface of the jettison tank. Mating can be a loose term in engineering but it is necessary to arrange that the tanks stayed securely fixed to the fuselage and at the same time the mushroom valve and seat met in a perfect contact otherwise fuel did not flow upwards to the carburettor. As each aircraft was brought to the stage where engines could be run, again after dark, each was towed "topside" on deck and put through its paces. A cock provided selection from main fuel to auxiliary fuel and it seemed logical to expect that fluid should flow. But almost as soon as the cock was turned, a small red light indicated lack of fuel pressure. And try as we may, it was a hit and miss affair to arrange the tank and valve position to work with much measure of success.

'After its engine had been run, and the fitters knew whether or not the slipper tank would feed properly, each fighter was given over to the armourers who jacked up into a flight attitude for harmonisation of the guns with the gunsight.'

Still the slipper tanks gave considerable trouble; they were the first of their type ever made, they had been designed and manufactured in a hurry – and it showed. During the early hours of 27 February HMS *Eagle* left Gibraltar with her precious cargo, escorted by a battle group which included the carrier *Argus*, a battleship, a cruiser and nine destroyers. That first attempt to deliver Spitfires to Malta was a failure. Flt Lt Stanley Grant, who was to

lead the fighters to the island, explained why to the author:

'The next day when we were well clear of land Hughes brought the aircraft up on deck to run the engines and, above all, to test the functioning of the long range tanks without which the operation was not on. These first 90gal tanks had evidently been produced in a great hurry and were "a bit of a lash-up". The fuel was drawn up into the main tanks by suction and if there was the slightest air leak in the seal between the tank and the fuselage, there was no transfer.

'Hughes soon found that the seals were not satisfactory and although he and his team strove hard all that day and well into the night he could not make them work properly. Accordingly, around midnight, with our take-off due the next morning. Hughes sent a message to the Admiral via Wg Cdr Maclean, saying that the aircraft could not be allowed to take off without further extensive tests. And since his men had now been working for over 20hr without rest they could not continue without some sleep. We heard later that the Admiral nearly exploded, and sent back the message that under no circumstances could his ships hang around in daylight in the middle of the Mediterranean, within easy range of enemy bombers. The Spitfires had to take off the next morning – at all costs. But Hughes was adamant. The aircraft were, in his view, not serviceable and he would not agree to their take-off until he was certain that the tanks would work. So the Admiral had to give in, and the whole fleet turned around and steamed back to Gibraltar.'

Once back at Gibraltar, there was hectic activity to get the Spitfire's new fuel tanks to work properly. Ray Honeybone recalled:

'Our worst enemy was the suction valve on the belly tanks; we had about a 95% failure rate with them . . . In the end a man from Supermarine was flown to Gibraltar to help us get them to work. When I met him I put up a bit of a black, I said the man who designed that system ought to jump off Beachy Head! He said "Don't say that, Corporal, I designed it . . .".'

As soon as he saw one of the tanks on HMS *Eagle,* the designer was able to pinpoint the reason why so many of them failed to work properly. Although it was vitally important to establish a good seal between the tank and the fuselage of the fighter, there was another problem that had not been realised. At the lowest point of each tank there was a small bulbous protrusion that acted as a sump, and the fuel transfer pipe reached almost to the bottom of that sump. If the sump was dented, that could block the end of the pipe and so prevent fuel transfer. In the course of crating, uncrating, and fitting the tanks to the aircraft by people unfamiliar with them, several of the tanks had dented

sumps. The remedy was to cut away the dented area and solder a patch over the cut-away area. That cured the problem, and there was a maximum effort to repair all of the damaged tanks and prove that they transferred fuel satisfactorily.

Early on the morning of 5 March, HMS *Eagle* and her covering force put to sea again. Once the ships were clear of land, the Spitfires were brought out on deck and their engines started. And this time all of the fuel tanks functioned perfectly. Then each fighter in turn was pointed in a safe direction and the armourers fired short bursts to test the guns.

Soon after dawn on the morning of the 7th, HMS *Eagle* reached the planned launching position. She turned into wind and Stanley Grant led the first of the Spitfires off the deck. At measured intervals the other 14 followed him into the air (the 16th Spitfire, it will be remembered, had been cannibalised to provide spares for the others).

Operation 'Spotter' was, on several counts, a remarkable operation. None of the pilots taking part in it had previously taken off from the deck of an aircraft carrier. There had been no opportunity to test fly the planes after re-assembly – the flight to Malta constituted the test flight, and if any part of the work had been done incorrectly a pilot might pay for the error with his life. Moreover, because re-assembly had taken place aboard the aircraft carrier, the Spitfires' compasses could not be 'swung' to determine their errors; the planes' compasses might give readings several degrees out and were not to be trusted, especially during a long oversea flight. Because of this, a Blenheim made a rendezvous with the carrier off Algeria and led the formation of fighters to Malta. Furthermore, it has to be remembered that as well as flying a distance greater than any previously attempted in a fighter version of the Spitfire, at the end of it the pilots might have to fight their way through to the airfields where they needed to land.

In spite of the difficulties, all 15 Spitfires did reach Malta safely and the next day they went into action. Four days after his arrival on the island, on the 11th, Stanley Grant was appointed commander of No 249 Squadron. By 25 March his victory score stood at one Messerschmitt Bf109 destroyed, another probably destroyed and a Junkers Ju87 damaged.

During March, HMS *Eagle* made two further deliveries of Spitfires to Malta. Using *Eagle* and other carriers, these operations would be repeated at regular intervals throughout the spring, summer and autumn of 1942. By the end of October, when the seige of the island was finally lifted, a total of 385 of these fighters had taken off from carriers and set course for Malta; 367 of them reached the island. These Spitfires would turn the tide of the air battle over Malta. Never again would the island be in as great a jeopardy as she was when the first of them landed here.

14 Battle in the Stratosphere

In August 1942 a Luftwaffe unit formed at Beauvais in northern France in readiness for a new series of bombing attacks on England: the Hoehenkampfkommando *(High Altitude Bomber Detachment). With German cities coming under increasingly heavy attack from the Royal Air Force, that nation's leaders judged it vitally important to deliver some form of retaliation, if only for propaganda purposes. Conventional bomber attacks by day or night suffered heavy losses from the steadily improving defences. Now the Luftwaffe was to try a new type of attack – from ultra high altitude.*

The *Hoehenkampfkommando* was a small unit, but it was rich in technical interest. It would receive only two Junkers Ju86Rs, but these bombers had been designed and built specially for operations above 40,000ft. This aircraft was powered by two Jumo 207 compression-ignition diesel engines, with turbo superchargers and nitrous oxide injection to provide maximum power at high altitude. The two-man crew was ensconced in a fully pressurised cabin, enabling them to work effectively for long periods at the ultra-high altitude. With a long narrow wing spanning 105ft,

the plane exceeded 45,000ft during test flights and had a maximum speed of just over 200mph. Given the technical cleverness of the Ju86R, it might seem carping to mention that it could carry only a single 550lb bomb to such an altitude. But, as has been said, the main consideration in mounting these attacks was to derive the maximum possible propaganda value from daylight attacks against which the defenders had no answer.

The new bombers delivered their first attacks on 24 August. Both Ju86Rs took part, one bombed Camberley and the other bombed Southampton. Fighter Command scrambled 15 Spitfires, all Mk Vs, to engage the intruders, but none of them got into a firing position.

That evening the German propaganda ministry jubilantly announced the daylight revenge attack by the *Hoehenkampfkommando*. There was no mention of the fact

Below:
Junkers Ju86R stratospheric bomber, similar to the aircraft involved in the action on 12 September 1942.

that only two aircraft were involved, or that they each dropped only one bomb.

On the following day one of the bombers was over England again. This time, more confident of their immunity to interception, the German crew flew a meandering course that took them over Southampton and north of London. They deposited their bomb on Stansted, flew down the east side of London and left the coast at Shoreham. This time nine Spitfires were scrambled, again Mk Vs, and again they failed to get anywhere near the intruder.

During the next two and a half weeks the Ju86Rs flew nine more sorties over England. On 29 August a couple of Spitfire Mk VIs of No 124 Squadron were among the fighters that attempted to intercept the high-flying bomber, but they had no more success than the others.

Meanwhile the nature of the new threat had become clear and Fighter Command was developing its own response. At Northolt a new unit, the Special Service Flight, was formed with specially modified Spitfire Mk IXs to counter the new menace. Plt Off Prince Emanuel Galitzine, a Russian émigré who had come to England as a child in 1919, was one of the pilots who volunteered for the new unit.

Early in September the first of the modified Spitfire Mk IXs arrived at the unit. Galitzine described the aircraft:

'The aircraft, serial BF273, had been lightened in almost every way possible. A lighter wooden propeller had been substituted for the normal metal one; all of the armour had been removed as had the four machine guns, leaving an armament of only the two 20mm Hispano cannons; the aircraft was painted in a special lightweight finish, which gave it a colour rather like Cambridge blue; and all equipment not strictly necessary for high altitude fighting was removed. It had the normal, not the extended span, wingtips. Of course, a pressure cabin would have been very nice;

but the Spitfire VII, which was in effect a Mk IX with a pressure cabin, was not yet ready for operations.

'On September 10th I made my first flight in the modified Spitfire IX and found it absolutely delightful to handle; during the war I flew 11 different versions of the Spitfire and this was far and away the best. The 450lb reduction in weight was immediately noticeable once one was airborne, and with the Merlin 61 she had plenty of power and was very lively. I made a second flight that day to test the cannons, during which I took her up to 43,400ft.'

Two days later Galitzine was again airborne in the modified Mk IX, this time in earnest. At 09.27hrs he was scrambled to intercept an aircraft detected on radar climbing to high altitude over northern France. That was the standard tactic used by the Junkers Ju88Rs, to get to high altitude before they crossed the south coast of England.

Galitzine spiralled up to 15,000ft over Northolt, then the ground controller informed him that the intruder was midway across the Channel heading for the Portsmouth area. The Spitfire turned to the southwest and continued its climb. As he approached the Solent at 40,000ft, Galitzine caught sight of the enemy plane slightly higher and to his starboard.

'I continued my climb and headed after him, closing in until I could make out the outline of a Junkers 86; by then I was about half-a-mile away from him and we were both at 42,000ft to the north of Southampton. The German crew had obviously seen me, because I saw the Junkers jettison its bomb, put up its nose to gain altitude and turn round for home. My Spitfire had plenty of performance in hand, however. I jettisoned my 30gal slipper tank which was now empty, and had little difficulty in following him in the climb and getting about 200ft above the bomber.'

Oberfeldwebel Horst Goetz, the pilot of the German bomber, now gives us his side of the story:

'Suddenly Erich [Leutnant Erich Sommer], sitting on my right, said that there was a fighter closing in from his side. I thought there was nothing remarkable about that – almost every time we had been over England in the Ju86, fighters had tried to intercept us. Then he said the fighter was climbing very fast and was nearly at our altitude. The next thing, it was above us. I thought Erich's eyes must be playing him tricks, so I leaned over to his side of the cabin to see for myself. To my horror I saw the Spitfire, a little above us and still climbing.'

Goetz immediately jettisoned the bomb, switched in full nitrous oxide injection and partially de-pressurised the cabin to reduce the risk of an explosion if it was punctured. He then pushed open the throttles to try to out-climb his would-be assailant.

To the Spitfire pilot, the German bomber seemed enormous and the long curling condensation trail behind it looked like the wake from a large liner ploughing through a calm sea at speed. Galitzine continued:

'I positioned myself for an attack and dived to about 200yd astern of him, where I opened up with a three-second burst. At the end of the burst my port cannon jammed and the Spitfire slewed round to starboard; then, as I passed through the bomber's slipstream, my canopy misted over. The canopy took about a minute to clear completely, during which time I climbed back into position for the next attack. When I next saw the Junkers it was heading southwards, trying to escape out to sea. I knew I had to get right in close behind him if I was to stand any chance of scoring hits, because it would be difficult to hold the Spitfire straight when the starboard cannon fired and she went into a yaw. Again I dived to attack but when I was about 100yd away the bomber went into a surprisingly tight turn to starboard. I opened fire but the Spitfire went into a yaw and fell out of the sky; I broke off the attack, turned outside him and climbed back to 44,000ft.'

Goetz managed to avoid two further attacks, then he made good his escape in a patch of mist. Galitzine broke off the

action and, now short of fuel, landed at Tangmere.

Goetz put the Junkers Ju86R down at Caen and the crew made a careful examination of the aircraft for damage. They found that it had been hit by just one round, which entered the top of the port wing and exited through the leading edge. The two men had indeed been fortunate to escape, and it was clear that the high-flying bombers' immunity from fighter attack was at an end. Less than three weeks after they started, the operations of the *Hoehen-kampfkommando* were brought to a precipitate end.

While conducting interviews in Germany, the author met Horst Goetz and Erich Sommer, and was able to bring them together with Emanuel Galitzine. After their meeting Goetz commented, tongue firmly in cheek: 'Emanuel and I have talked about our battle in great detail and now we understand each other's problems. The next time we fly against each other, we shall be able to do things better!'

Top and above left:
Hole through the wing of the Ju86R from rear to front, caused by an armour-piercing round from Galitzine's cannon. *Goetz*

Left:
Horst Goetz (left) and Emanuel Galitzine pictured after being brought together by the author, going through their unique air combat.

15 More Spitfires in Captivity

This page:
Spitfire PR IF in German markings. The identification of the aircraft and the circumstances of its capture are not known.

This page:
In October 1943 German forces captured their largest haul of intact Spitfires when they seized the island of Kos. Two squadrons of Spitfire Vs, No 7 (South African Air Force) and No 74, were based there. Several of the fighters were damaged in air attacks, and the remainder were prevented from getting airborne by cratering of the runway and seeding of the airfield at Antimachia with anti-personnel bomblets. It is believed that at least six Spitfires were captured intact. These German photographs show some of the aircraft, one having its engine run. It is not known whether any of the fighters were taken off the island. *via Willis*

Above:
This PR Mk XI served for several months with the Circus Rosarius, a Luftwaffe unit which flew demonstrations with captured enemy planes. *via Griehl*

Left:
Not what they might appear: a formation of clipped winged Spitfire XVIs of No 17 Squadron wearing German markings with yellow noses, to play the part of Bf109s in one of the set-piece items during the RAF Display at Farnborough in July 1950.
Charles E. Brown, RAF Museum

Left:
Spitfire V flown by Wg Cdr Stefan Witozenc, commander of the 2nd Polish Fighter Wing, in July 1942. The white stripes were painted on the cowling as a means of identifying the formation leader. *Cynk*

Top:
Wg Cdr 'Johnny' Johnson, commander of the Kenley Wing in 1943, pictured with his personal Mk IX EN398. *RAF Museum*

Above:
Mk IX of Sqn Ldr James Storrar, commander of No 65 Squadron from January to November 1943. *RAF Museum*

Right:
Spitfire IX wearing the VY identification letters of Wg Cdr Adolphe Vybiral, commander of No 134 (Czech) Fighter Wing in 1944. *IWM*

This page:
This silver Mk VIII of No 549 Squadron, ZF-Z, carried the personal badge of Sqn Ldr David Glaser (seated on side of cockpit). The unit operated from airfields in the Northern Territories of Australia during the final stages of the Pacific war. *Glaser*

17 D-Day Top Cover Squadron

Having flown Spitfire Mk Vs in combat over Malta, Flg Off Don Nicholson returned to England at the end of 1943 and joined No 131 Squadron at Colerne in Wiltshire operating the Mk IX. At the beginning of March 1944 the unit re-equipped with Spitfire VIIs, the specialised high altitude version fitted with a pressurised cabin, an uprated Merlin and extended wingtips to enable it to operate above 40,000ft.

To provide sufficient fuel for a full throttle climb to such an altitude, and a useful endurance when the fighter got there, the Mk VII was fitted with enlarged main tanks holding 96gal of fuel, and two 14gal tanks in the leading edge of the wings. The Mk VII thus had an internal fuel capacity of 124gal - 40% more than other Merlin-engined fighter versions of the Spitfire operating from Britain (the Mk VIII had a similar tank arrangement, but all squadrons with this version were based overseas).

By the beginning of 1944 it was rare for German aircraft to attempt bombing or reconnaissance missions over England at extreme altitude, and No 131 Squadron had no opportunity to use the Mk VII in its designed role as a high altitude interceptor. The squadron would be able to put to good use the extended range capability which came with this little-known version of the Spitfire, however.

It took the pilots of No 131 Squadron only a few days to convert from the Mk IX Spitfire to the Mk VII. Don Nicholson remembered the new version with affection:

'The Mk VII was designed for high altitude operations and our planes wore high altitude camouflage, light grey on top and blue grey underneath. I liked the Mk VII, it was a good aeroplane. The highest I ever took one was to 39,000ft; it could have continued climbing, but I had no reason to go any higher.'

On 18 March 1944 Nicholson flew his first mission in the new version, when the squadron put up eight Spitfire VIIs to escort a force of Mosquitoes attacking a target south of Dieppe. The raiders were engaged by flak, but no enemy fighters appeared and all planes returned safely.

At the beginning of March the squadron moved to Harrowbeer near Plymouth for a brief spell. There it got its first taste of the type of operation that would become its main task during the run up to the forthcoming invasion of Normandy: that of flying high level patrols over ports along the southwest coast of England, where the ships were assembling for the operation. Nicholson continued:

'Our job was to prevent German reconnaissance planes taking photographs of the ports. They made few attempts to send in reconnaissance planes; we chased them on one or two occasions but by the time we reached their level they had gone.'

Late in May, No 131 Squadron moved to Culmhead near Taunton, where it joined No 616 Squadron also operating Spitfire

VIIs. This airfield was to serve as base for the Mk VII Wing during the invasion period. Events were now moving to a climax, and Don Nicholson was treated to a grandstand view of the proceedings:

'On 1st, 2nd, 4th, and three times on 5th June I took part in patrols to protect the invasion ships, flying up and down between Portland Bill and Star Point at 22,000ft. Below us, off Portland Bill and in Lyme Bay, were hundreds of ships of all sizes and types.

'The term "Top cover" was relative. If there was need for high cover, we would provide it. If there were other marks of Spitfire also flying cover for the convey, they would be at 10,000 or 15,000ft and we would be above them. But the Germans were not coming in at high altitude, we were often used as an ordinary Spitfire squadron.'

As if to emphasise No 131 Squadron's 'ordinariness', on the morning of D-Day, 6 June, the unit was ordered to send eight Mk VIIs on a low level armed reconnaissance of the Brest Peninsula. The Spitfires

Right:
Flg Off Don Nicholson of No 131 Squadron in his Spitfire VII. *Nicholson*

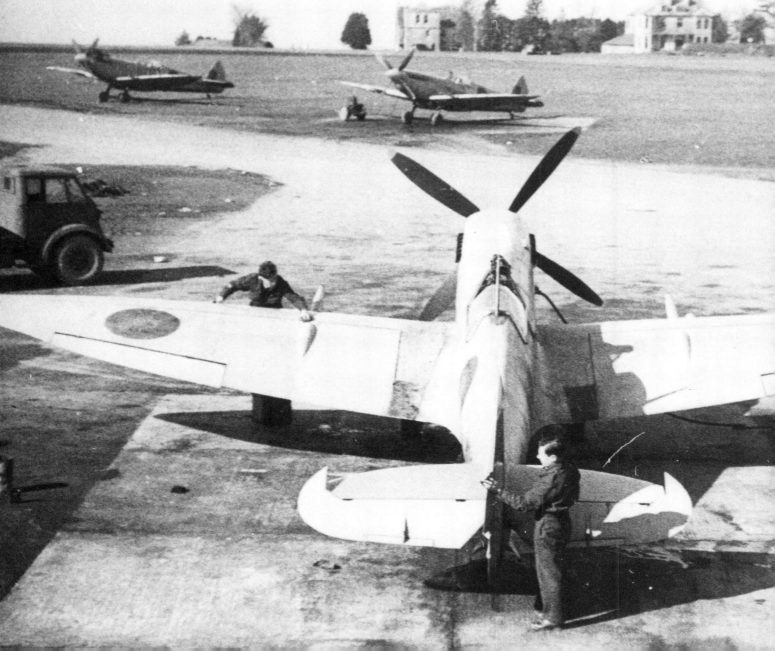

This page:
Photographs of Spitfire VIIs bearing the markings of operational units are rare, which makes these of Don Nicholson's aircraft, NX-L MD172, all the more interesting. The pictures show clearly the intake scoop for the cabin blower, on the starboard side of the nose below the exhausts, a recognition feature of this pressurised fighter. The shots were taken shortly before D-Day and the application of invasion markings. *Nicholson*

found and strafed three trains, two trucks and two cars, and returned without loss.

In the days following the invasion the squadron settled down to a routine of patrols to cover the beach-head and shipping off the coast, punctuated with an offensive fighter sweep over northern France on most days. On 10 June eight Spitfires on a sweep near Loudeac found a goods train with some 20 freight wagons covered with camouflage netting. Four of the fighters flew in line abreast to strafe the train from abeam, while the other four flew top cover. The attack left the locomotive enveloped in dense smoke and several wagons on fire.

On 12 June Nos 131 and 616 Squadrons mounted a 24-Spitfire 'Rodeo' operation against the German airfield at Le Mans. While the No 616 provided top cover, No 131 Squadron strafed the airfield. Two enemy fighters were set on fire and others damaged. Intensive light flak greeted the attackers, and as he came off the airfield Flt Lt Moody went into a steep climb and called on the radio to say he was bailing out. Nothing more was heard from him. Two other Spitfires took hits but were able to continue with the operation. The squadrons reformed and flew to Laval airfield where the tactics were repeated, this time with No 616 Squadron doing the strafing and No 131 providing cover. Flg Off Ken Parry spotted a Messerschmitt Bf109 flying low to the west of the airfield, and he and his wing man pounced on it and shot it down.

Returning from Laval Flg Off 'Eddy' Edwards ran short of fuel, so he put down in the beach-head area at a small landing ground near St Mere Eglise. Used only by light spotting planes, the airfield had no supply of 100 octane petrol. So American soldiers helped Edwards syphon fuel from a fighter which had made a wheels up landing nearby. Later that afternoon the Spitfire was able to take off and return to Culmhead.

Early on the morning of 15th, Don Nicholson set out from Culmhead for a mission that would prove all too exciting. With Flg Off Edwards as wing-man, he had been briefed to fly a low level visual reconnaissance to St Peter Port, Guernsey, to follow up an intelligence report that a U-boat had arrived in the port:

'We were tasked to have a look at St Peter Port to see if the sub was there. Trying to maintain the element of surprise we flew out at low level and went past the west of the island as if we were going to France. Then we cut back and came up the east side of the island on the deck. While my No 2 stayed out to sea covering me, I roared over the harbour wall at about 50ft. And there sitting in the harbour was the U-boat, firing at me with everything he had!

'Suddenly the plane juddered and I knew it had been hit; I saw a couple of bullet holes in the wings. And immediately afterwards it was clear I had lost my wireless and rudder trim. I jinked to throw the gunners off their aim and headed out to sea, keeping low and trying to make the most of the available cover.

'As I came out my No 2 closed on me. He could see I was damaged, he waggled his wings and led me home. It was a good thing he was with me, because by the time we reached the coast of England our airfield at Culmhead was fogged in and we had to divert to Harrowbeer. Apart from the lack of rudder trim, the Spit handled normally.'

On the ground at Harrowbeer, Nicholson inspected the damage. A couple of rifle calibre bullets had passed through the starboard wing without hitting anything vital. More seriously, a 20mm round had exploded on the starboard side of the fuselage just aft of the cockpit. On detonating, the explosive shell had blown a hole the size of man's fist and the blast sent splinters flying in all directions. Several went clean through the port side of the fuselage, others caused internal damage and wrecked the radio and severed the rudder trim cable. Following an engineering examination the Spitfire, MD172, was judged beyond economical repair and written off.

Later that afternoon the squadron put up a four-aircraft sweep of the area around Rennes, and claimed the destruction of 10 supply trucks.

During the 17th, Flt Lt Rudland and Flg Off Parry flew a comparative trial with two Spitfire VIIs, one with rounded wing tips and the other with the pointed tips fitted to the rest of the squadron's Spitfires. The trial established that the rounded tips were the better for operations at low and medium altitudes, and in the days that followed these were fitted to all aircraft. The pointed wing tips, which had been one of the main recognition features of the Mk VII, saw little further use.

Right:
Sqn Ldr James O'Meara, the commander of No 131 Squadron, in his Spitfire 'Spirit of Kent'. The squadron had been adopted by the county of Kent and its badge incorporated the white horse of the county. *Nicholson*

At first light on 18 June the squadron sent eight aircraft on an armed shipping reconnaissance around the Channel Islands. South of Jersey the fighters found two large self-propelled barges, on which they carried out repeated strafing runs. Several hits were scored, and when the Spitfires left the scene both vessels were stopped and one was on fire. During a 'Rhubarb' mission over Northern France later that day, the Spitfires shot up four motor vehicles.

On the 19th Flg Off Edwards was flying on a sweep with No 616 Squadron near Mayenne when there was a rare encounter with German fighters. In the mêlée that followed Edwards shot down a Messerschmitt Bf109.

On 20 June the squadron sent 10 Spitfires, each with 90gal slipper tank, for a 'Rhubarb' fighter sweep operation over northwest France. They were to have gone deeper, but south of Rennes a blanket of thick cloud covered the ground. The formation was forced to turn back without engaging ground targets.

On the 21st WO Crayford and Flt Sgt Tanner conducted a low altitude shipping reconnaissance around Guernsey and near St Peter Port they came under intense and accurate flak. Tanner's aircraft was hit, but he managed to get it across the Channel and made a wheels-up landing at Bolt Head airfield.

On the 22nd, the squadron put up 12 Spitfires to escort Lancasters attacking targets in the St Omer area; the mission was flown without incident.

For the rest of June and the first week of July No 131 Squadron continued with its routine of fighter sweeps over northern France, the occasional escort mission and

Right and below:
Don Nicholson's aircraft NX-L pictured after it was hit by flak over Guernsey on 15 June 1944. The 20mm high explosive round struck the starboard side of the fuselage and detonated, causing severe internal damage and a mass of splinter holes on the port side. The Spitfire never flew again. Note the crude application of the invasion stripes.

frequent, if invariably uneventful, defensive patrols over the beach head area.

On 8 July, No 131 Squadron exploited its extended range capability for the first time. Each carrying a 90gal tank, the 12 Spitfires flew a 'Rhubarb' sweep to Tours. The force strafed oil tanks, a truck and a couple of cars. No enemy fighters were encountered, and the fighters all landed at Culmhead after 3hr 20min airborne.

On 12 July, Wg Cdr Peter Brothers led the Spitfire VIIs of both Culmhead squadrons to Ford airfield in Sussex, where they refuelled and took off to escort Lancasters attacking the Vaires-sur-Marne marshalling yard east of Paris. The mission was uneventful.

During the next couple of weeks the squadron's operations were confined mainly to the shorter range sweeps. Then on 27 July the Spitfires went deep into western France, to the Poitiers area. The area was a hunting ground for fighter-bombers operating from airfields in the beach-head, however, and there was little to be found. Except for an attack on a single lorry near Tours, which was damaged, the mission was uneventful.

Early in August German fighters put in a few brief appearances over western France. During a long range sweep to Tours by 12 Spitfires on the 6th, the squadron encountered a force of FW190s and claimed two shot down; on the following day, in the same area, there was another dogfight in which three more FW190s were claimed. No Spitfires were lost or damaged in either engagement.

On 11 August the squadron mounted what was to be its longest ranging operation of all, a round trip of 690 miles to escort Lancasters attacking the submarine pens at La Pallice. The Spitfires were airborne for 3hr 50min, as Don Nicholson well remembers:

'Three hours 50min – that's a long time to sit in a Spit, believe you me! It was very

79

tiring, just sitting there. We went as high level escort at about 25,000ft, way above the Lancs who were down at about 18,000ft. We flew throttled well back, we had to be careful with the fuel or we would run out. We didn't have enough fuel for a fight. Had there been a real shindig at the target, we would have been likely to run out of fuel on the way back. We just had to hope that nothing like that would happen.'

Fortunately for the pilots of the escorting Spitfires, German fighters did not attempt to contest the incursion.

From the middle of August, as the Allied armies forced the Germans out of France, No 131 Squadron shifted its main area of operations to the skies over Holland, Belgium and, finally, to Germany itself. The new phase began on the 15th, when the unit staged through Manston to escort Lancasters attacking Le Ceulot airfield near Brussels.

At the end of August No 131 Squadron moved to Friston in Sussex, to bring it closer to its new operating area. On 3 September its Spitfires escorted Lancasters attacking the airfield at Deelen in Holland. On the 6th the squadron staged through Coltishall for its first mission over Germany, to Emden in support of 160 Lancasters and Halifaxes attacking the port installations. On the 11th it supported bombers raiding Gelsenkirchen in the Ruhr Valley. Two days later the squadron penetrated still deeper into the enemy homeland when it escorted Lancasters to Osnabrück, in a mission lasting 3hr 10min.

On 17 September the Mk VIIs provided top cover for the Allied airborne landings at Grave, Nijmegen and Arnhem in Holland. On the 30th the unit escorted Marauders attacking a target near Arnhem. As was the case on every deep penetration escort mission mounted by No 131 Squadron, no enemy fighters were encountered. But on the 30th the squadron suffered the rare loss of an aircraft, when Flg Off Baxter had an engine failure and was forced to land in a ploughed field near Brussels. Unhurt, the pilot returned to the squadron a few days later.

The pace of operations continued throughout October, with the squadron providing escorts for bombers attacking targets at Arnhem, Nijmegen, Deventer and Walcheren Island in Holland, and Wanne Eiekel in Germany. On the last day of the month the unit was ordered to cease operations, pending transfer of its personnel to India where it was intended to reform the squadron with Spitfire VIIIs. The re-equipment was not complete when the war ended in the Far East, however, and No 131 Squadron saw no further action.

18 Gyro Gunsight — The Great Leveller

At the end of 1943 the RAF introduced an important new type of gunsight: the Gyro Gunsight Mk IID. The result of more than three years' hard and often inspired work at the Royal Aircraft Establishment at Farnborough, the gyro gunsight was designed to calculate the amount ahead of the target — the deflection angle — a gunner needed to aim in order to secure hits. The ability to work out the deflection angle instinctively during a high speed turning combat, using a fixed graticule sight, had been mastered by a few fighter aces. But the necessary mental gymnastics were beyond the ability of average squadron pilots, who were unable to score hits in such combats except from very short ranges. With the gyro gunsight, the average pilot could shoot at large angles of deflection as accurately as the aces.

The gyro gunsight worked on the principle that if a fighter pilot held a turning enemy aircraft in his sight as he followed its turn, the rate of turn of his aircraft was proportional to the deflection angle required to hit the enemy. A gyroscope fitted in the new sight measured the rate of turn and was arranged to tilt a mirror, which adjusted the position of the sighting graticule to give the required deflection angle. The amount of deflection required varied with range, however, so the deflection angle thus found was correct for only one value of range. To overcome this problem the gunsight was fitted with a simple system for optical rangefinding. As he went into action the pilot would set on the sight the wingspan of the enemy aircraft he was engaging. Then, as he closed on the enemy plane, the pilot continually turned a separate control on the throttle arm to adjust the size of the gunsight graticule so that it was the same apparent size as the wingspan of the enemy plane. Since the wingspan of the target aircraft was set on the sight, the adjustment of the graticule in this way 'told' the gunsight the range of the target throughout the engagement. A simple analogue system in the gunsight then calculated the amount of deflection needed.

Right and overleaf:
Gyro Gunsight installed in a Spitfire IX.
Murland

Once fighter pilots got used to the new sight and learned of its foibles, the accuracy of their deflection shooting improved dramatically. During 1944 an analysis of 130 combats by Spitfire IXs fitted with the old fixed-graticule sights revealed 34 kills — 26% of the total. During the same period, one squadron operating the same version of the Spitfire fitted with the new gunsight was involved in 38 combats during which it secured 19 kills — 50% of the total. The new type of sight had almost doubled the effectiveness of air-to-air gunnery and pilots reported scoring hits on evading targets at ranges as great as 600yd and deflection angles of up to 50°. Fortunately for the Allies the German equivalent of the gyro gunsight, the Askania EZ42, did not progress beyond the service trials stage before the war ended.

It is difficult to exaggerate the significance of the gyro gunsight in the Allies' maintenance of air superiority during the final year of the war, when Spitfires and other piston-engined fighters had to fight the much faster German jet planes. The new-found improvement in the accuracy of air-to-air gunnery did much to compensate for the huge difference in performance, enabling Allied fighters to shoot down two German jet fighters for each Allied fighter or bomber destroyed by the jets.

For a Spitfire to catch a German jet the former usually needed the advantage of altitude and surprise — and a large measure of luck. The first such action occurred over Holland on 5 October 1944, and involved a dozen Spitfire IXs of No 401 (Canadian) Squadron. Flt Lt Roderick Smith, leading the patrol, afterwards reported:

'I was leading 401 Squadron at 13,000ft in the Nijmegen area about 5 miles NE of the bridge. We were flying on a NE course when I sighted an Me262 coming head on 500 below. He went into a port climbing turn and I turned starboard after him with several other Spitfires chasing him. He then dived down towards the bridge, twisting and turning and half rolling at very high speed. He then flew across Nijmegen turning from side to side. I saw a Spitfire get some strikes on him and he streamed white smoke from the starboard wing root. He flew on at very high speed still and I managed to get behind him and fire two 3sec bursts at 200-300yd approx. He zoomed very high and I saw strikes on him in the port and starboard nacelles. A small fire started in the starboard nacelle and a big one on the port nacelle while I was firing. I broke down to starboard under him and he turned down to starboard behind me. I thought at that time he was trying to attack me, even though in flames. He passed behind me and crashed in a field about 2 miles SW of Nijmegen . . .'

Smith, a veteran air fighter who had taken part in the defence of Malta and who already had a dozen kills to his credit, was an accomplished deflection-shooter and although his fighter was fitted with a gyro gunsight he did not use it. He judged the deflection angle for himself and left the sighting graticule in the fixed position.

Three of the other pilots in the squadron, less experienced than their leader, made full use of the new sight and there is evidence that they secured the long range hits on the German jet fighter. Flg Off John MacKay:

'Flying Red 4 to F/L Everard when we sighted the Me262. I followed Red 3 (F/L Everard) into the attack. After a complete spiral turn F/L Everard was slightly out of position and told me to go in to attack. I got on the tail of the Me262 following it down to the ground, firing whenever I could get my sight on the A/C. Saw strikes on the after part of the fuselage and the port or starboard wing root. The A/C was extremely manoeuvrable. The pilot was hot and put the A/C through everything in the book. We were about 2,000 to 3,000 when S/L Smith came into attack. The starboard nacelle broke into flames, the aircraft pulled up to the right and then dove down (burning) on a Spit (S/L Smith) seeming to want to ram the Spitfire. The Me262 then crashed into the deck. GGS II used. For this I claim 1/5 Me262 destroyed.'

Flg Off Gus Sinclair:
'I was flying as Blue 1 in 401 Blackout Squadron when squadron spotted an Me262 at about 12,000 NE of Nijmegen. Red Section fired first, bringing the Me262 across the front of Blue Section. I turned in behind and fired 4 or 5sec bursts, saw strikes but was crowded out by two other A/C coming in from above; this A/C was destroyed immediately after. Strikes were observed along the wings and fuselage.

Before making my attack I observed strikes or pieces flying off from the attacks made from Red Section. This A/C dived and turned down to the deck, the turns were very tight. I used cine gun and new gyro sight. I claim 1/5 Me262 destroyed.'

Flt Lt 'Tex' Davenport:
'I was flying as Yellow 1, 401 Blackout Squadron when we sighted an Me262 at 12,000 5 miles NE Nijmegen. There was a great mix-up as all 12 Spits dove for the jet job, I waited until he made his first break then came in 20° line astern at approx 450mph. I gave a 3sec burst at 400yd and observed strikes in fuselage. I then continued the chase which was composed of rolls, dives and turns at approx 375mph. I finally closed into 300yd line astern and emptied the remainder of my guns, approx 10 or 12sec, into the kite, observing strikes all in engines and fuselage. The A/C was burning all this time. The pilot seemed to be unhurt and put up a good fight all during this, at the last realising the fight was up he attempted to ram Red 1 on the way to the ground when he crashed and burned. I used camera and got 8ft film, cannon, MG. Gyro sight functioned properly. No ammunition left. I claim 1/5 Me262 destroyed.'

The Messerschmitt Me262 belonged to a fighter-bomber unit — *5 Staffel* of *Kampfgeschwader 51*. The pilot who had put up such a stout fight, Hpt Hans-Christoff Buttmann, was killed when his aircraft dived into the ground.

Below:
Messerschmitt Me262 jet, similar to the aircraft shot down by Spitfires of No 401 Squadron near Nijmegen on 5 October 1944.

19 Wartime Round Up

Above:
The author is indebted to Ray Sturtivant for making available these extremely rare photos of the Spitfire PR XIII in squadron markings. Although the shots lack the sharpness normally required for publication in an Ian Allan book, these are permissible because such pictures have not previously been published. Only 26 Spitfires, Mk IIs, Mk Vs and Mk PR IGs, were modified into Mk XIIIs by the fitting of Merlin 32 engines; the four outer machine guns were retained. After a short and undistinguished operational career as a low altitude photographic reconnaissance aircraft, these machine were relegated to second line tasks. In 1944 six Mk XIIIs were issued to 718 Squadron, the Fleet Air Arm Army Co-operation Training Unit at Henstridge, and these are depicted. Examination of the original prints reveals that G3-K was R7335. *Sturtivant*

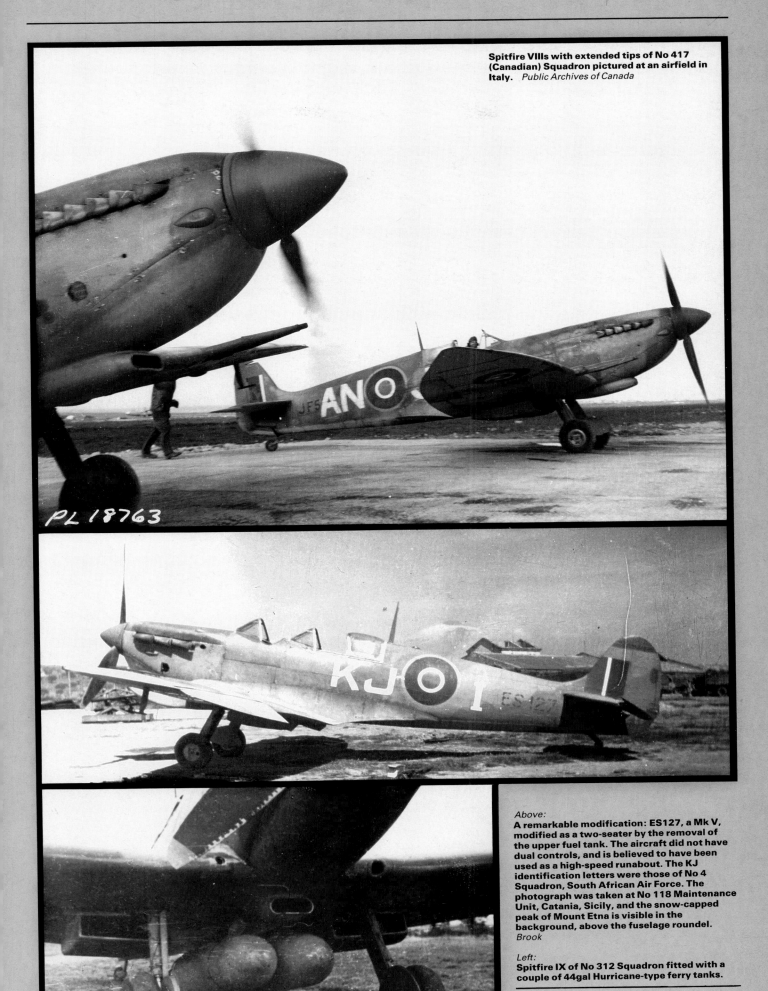

Spitfire VIIIs with extended tips of No 417 (Canadian) Squadron pictured at an airfield in Italy. *Public Archives of Canada*

PL18763

Above:
A remarkable modification: ES127, a Mk V, modified as a two-seater by the removal of the upper fuel tank. The aircraft did not have dual controls, and is believed to have been used as a high-speed runabout. The KJ identification letters were those of No 4 Squadron, South African Air Force. The photograph was taken at No 118 Maintenance Unit, Catania, Sicily, and the snow-capped peak of Mount Etna is visible in the background, above the fuselage roundel.
Brook

Left:
Spitfire IX of No 312 Squadron fitted with a couple of 44gal Hurricane-type ferry tanks.

MH819, an invasion-striped Mk IX of No 310
Squadron that was part of No 134 Wing,
pictured at Appledram in June 1944. The
aircraft is being levelled off in preparation for
gun harmonisation. *Hurt*

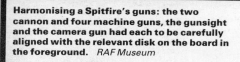

Harmonising a Spitfire's guns: the two
cannon and four machine guns, the gunsight
and the camera gun had each to be carefully
aligned with the relevant disk on the board in
the foreground. *RAF Museum*

20 Postwar Spitfires and Seafires

Above:
Final assembly of Spitfire FR18s at High Post late in 1945. *R. J. Mitchell Museum*

This page:
Spitfire F21s of No 41 Squadron operating from the airfield at Lübeck shortly after the end of the war. The two aircraft taxying out to take off each carry a rack with four 25lb practice bombs under the fuselage. *Adamson*

Above left:
Spitfire FR XIV of No 11 Squadron, based at Miho, Japan in 1946, pictured with Mount Fuji in the background. *via Arnold*

Left:
Line-up of clipped-wing Spitfire XIVEs of No 17 Squadron which was also based at Miho. RN135, bearing the squadron commander's pennant, was the mount of Sqn Ldr 'Ginger' Lacey. *via Arnold*

This page:
Spitfire IXs of No 73 Squadron pictured at Takali, Malta, in 1945. *Brook*

Top:
In November 1947 No 73 Squadron, at Takali, re-equipped with Spitfire F22s. It was to be the sole regular squadron to operate this version, and retained it for about a year before re-equipping with Vampires.
RAF Museum

Above:
Seafire LIIIs of 794 Squadron ranged on the deck of HMS *Implacable* early in 1947. The aircraft in the right foreground, A-114, was serial NF510. The aircraft carry the new postwar colour scheme, but with oversized fuselage roundels and tail letters. *Sturtivant*

Left:
A Seafire 17 comes to a steaming end on *Implacable's* deck after running into the barrier, July 1949. *Sturtivant*

21 Spitfires with Foreign Air Forces

Following the end of the war the RAF had vast numbers of Spitfires surplus to its diminishing requirement. During the years that followed many were sold or given to foreign air forces rebuilding themselves after the conflict. Apart from the air forces of the Commonwealth nations, those of France, Holland and Belgium, Denmark, Norway and Sweden, Portugal, Italy, and Czechoslovakia, Greece, Turkey and Egypt, Syria, Eire and Thailand, Israel and Burma all operated Spitfires or Seafires in frontline units during the postwar period.

In this section we look at Spitfires that went into operation with the Belgian, Dutch and Czechoslovakian Air Forces, at the resale of several of the Czechoslovakian Spitfires to Israel in 1948, and at the subsequent resale of some of the Israeli Spitfires to Burma 1954.

With the Belgian Air Force

Below:
Belgian Air Force Mk IXs, their armament removed, operating from the Ecole de Chasse at Coxyde. *via Decobeck*

This page and overleaf:
After the war the Royal Belgian Air Force received 132 Spitfire F XIVs and FR XIVs from RAF stocks. The aircraft depicted belonged to No 350 Squadron (code letters MN) based at Beauvechain, the Ecole de Chasse (IQ) at Brustem and Coxyde, and the Escadrille Auxiliare (GV) at Beauvechain. *via Decobeck*

This disarmed Mark IX was registered
OO-ARA in 1956, and operated by the Belgian
Cogea Company under contract to the
government as a target towing aircraft. Note
the towing bar just visible under the rudder.
via Decobeck

With the Dutch Air Force

This page:
Mk IXs of the Fighter Training School (JVS) at Twente. Aircraft H-11 had previously been MJ642; H-4 had been MK962. *van der Meer*

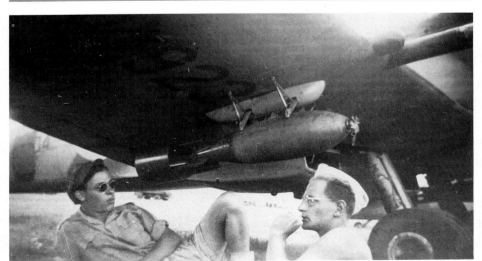

This page:
Mk IXs of No 322 Squadron being prepared for operations from Semarang in Java in 1949, during the war preceding the independence of the present state of Indonesia. H-63 had been MH725, H-61 had been MK923. *van der Meer*

Above right:
Spitfire from the JVS carrying out a low altitude bombing attack on the range near Twente. The target was a much-battered Messerschmitt Bf109. *van der Meer*

Right:
Orange painted two-seat Mk IX PH-NFN, ex-BS147, ex-H-99, operated by Schreiner Aero Contractors as a target tug. The aircraft served in this role from August 1955 to May 1957, when it suffered damage in an accident and was scrapped. *van der Meer*

With the Czech, Israeli and Burmese Air Forces

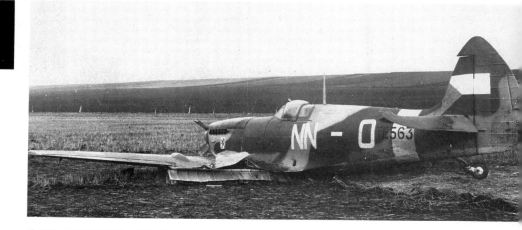

Top:
Spitfire IXs of No 310 Squadron at Manston in August 1945, pictured before setting out for Czechoslovakia. The aircraft carry no national marking on the fuselage. *Hurt*

Above:
Aircraft of the same unit drawn up for inspection at Prague/Ruzyne airfield on 18 August 1945, immediately after their arrival. *Hurt*

Centre right:
TE563 pictured after crash landing in Czechoslovakia late in 1945. *Hurt*

Right:
TE524 of the 5th Air Regiment of the Czechoslovakian Air Force in mid-1946. This aircraft had previously flown with No 312 Squadron and still carried the unit's badge on the cowling. *Hurt*

Top:
Mk IXs of the 7th Air Regiment pictured at Brno in 1946. *Hurt*

Above:
A-717 of the Leteca Vojenska Akademie, the Czech equivalent of the RAF's Central Flying School, pictured in 1948. The serial number MH758 is painted on the fin, and the aircraft retained the badge of No 312 Squadron on the nose. *Hurt*

Left:
During 1948 the Czech government sold some 50 Spitfire IXs to the Israeli Air Force where these, and others later acquired from Italy, were flown in combat by the 101st Fighter Squadron depicted here. *via Arnold*

This page:

In 1954 the Spitfires became surplus to Israeli requirements, and after refurbishment about 30 were sold to the Burmese Air Force. These pictures were taken at Sharjah as the ex-RAF, ex-Czech or Italian, ex-Israeli planes were being delivered to their new owners.
via Arnold

22 Seafires over Korea — The Last of the Few

In January 1949 Seafire FR47 VR971 left the production line at South Marston, the last of more than 22,000 Spitfires and Seafires built. Only two front line Royal Navy units were to receive the Seafire FR47: 804 Squadron, which operated with it between January 1948 and August 1949; and 800 Squadron which flew this version between April 1949 and November 1950. When the Korean War broke out, 800 Squadron happened to be in the Far East, and the unit took part in the initial stages of the conflict. Tommy Handley would be the last man to command a frontline Seafire squadron flying from a carrier, and in this account he describes the unit's operations during the period before and during the Korean War.

During World War 2 Tommy Handley flew Seafires and Hellcats with front line units. After the war he remained in the Fleet Air Arm and in December 1949, with the rank of lieutenant, he was sent to the Supermarine works at Chilbolton for a short conversion course on the Seafire FR47. He found the Mk 47 a great improvement over previous versions of Seafire:

'The Seafire 47 was a superb aeroplane in the air. It was a better fighter than previous marks, could carry a greater weapon load and had a better range and endurance. The Rolls-Royce Griffon fitted with the injector pump was a most reliable engine, and the squadron experienced no engine failures of any kind. The contrarotating propellers were a big advance, and even at full throttle on take-off there was no tendency to swing. Also there was no change of rudder trim in a dive, which helped considerably when operating in the ground attack role.'

On completion of the conversion course at Chilbolton, Handley went to Royal Navy Air Station Sembawang, Singapore, to take up his appointment as Senior Pilot (deputy commander) of 800 Squadron. The unit had disembarked from the light fleet carrier HMS *Triumph* and its Seafire 47s were conducting air strikes on areas of the Malayan jungle where guerillas were thought to be operating.

'I flew only one of these sorties, on

Left:
Tommy Handley, whose account of Seafire operations over Korea appears below.
Handley

20 January 1950, when I was briefed to shoot up a 1,000yd grid square reference in the jungle. I fired eight 60lb rockets and 400 rounds of 20mm into it. I saw no results and nobody appeared to fire back.'

In February No 800 Squadron, together with 827 operating Fireflys, re-embarked in *Triumph*. During the next few months the carrier made a tour of the Far East, visiting Hong Kong and Japan. At each, the carrier's Air Group flew to a land base and carried on its training programme from there. There was a general reluctance by those in authority to fly the Seafire 47s from the carrier too often, the theory appeared to be that the less they flew the less would be written off or damaged:

'Seafires were not easy to deck land. The Mk 47 was a much heavier aircraft than the previous marks, and heavy landings often resulted in damaged oleo legs. Also the fuselage aft of the cockpit was not sufficiently strengthened to withstand anything but a near-perfect deck landing. The long sting hook made catching a wire reasonably easy, but if the landing was much off-centre or made with any skid or slip on, then the wire would shake the aircraft rather like a terrier shakes a rat. The result could be a wrinkling of the after fuselage section.'

During April, May and June 1950 Handley made only 26 deck landings, an average of about two per week. Most of his take-offs were unassisted runs off the deck. The catapult was used when there was a light wind, or if the presence of other aircraft on deck left insufficient room for a full take-off run.

Triumph's peacetime cruise came to a sudden and unexpected end on the morning of 25 June 1950, when North Korean troops stormed over the 38th Parallel and advanced into South Korea. On the 26th the US Navy was ordered to support the South Korean forces, and on the 27th the Royal Navy placed its warships in Japanese waters under the operational control of the US Navy. Escorted by the cruiser *Belfast* and two destroyers, HMS *Triumph* left Japan and arrived off the west coast of Korea on 2 July. There she joined US Navy Task Force 77 which included the carrier *Valley Forge*.

On the following morning the two carriers launched a joint strike against airfields in the Pyongyang area. It was the Seafire 47's first operational mission from a carrier and, as Handley explained, some of them had to use RATOG (rocket assisted take-off gear) to get airborne:

'For the strike we had a big range of aircraft on deck. On a small carrier like *Triumph* that meant the aircraft at the head of the range did not get a full take-off run. So the four Seafires at the front were fitted with RATOG. RATOG was not popular — carrier operations were hazardous enough, without having to rely on cordite and more electric circuitry. The technique was to fire the rockets late in the take-off run, as the aircraft passed a mark on the deck. Firing the rockets gave quite a push, though not as much as going off the catapult. Once airborne, the pilot would jettison the rocket packs. With free

YEAR 1950		AIRCRAFT		PILOT, OR 1ST PILOT	2ND PILOT, PUPIL OR PASSENGER	DUTY (INCLUDING RESULTS AND REMARKS)
MONTH	DATE	Type	No.			
						— TOTALS BROUGHT FORWARD
June	6	Seafire 47	459	Self.	—	Strike on Itazuke, Kyushu (c)
"	7	"	459	"	"	Strike on H.M.S. Belfast.
"	8	"	459	"	"	Strike on Triumph & Belfast.
"	13	"	459	"	"	F.D.X. & A.C.T. at Ominato Misawa
"	14	"	459	"	"	8° Verticals op Ominato. Beat up.
"	21	"	477	"	"	A.C.T. X. South of Kagayama
"	30	"	477	"	"	F.D.X at 28,000' Strike on Fleet
				800 Squadron 13th C.A.G. H.M.S. Triumph. Summary for June 1950 Seafire 47 " – April, May, June 1950. "		
				[signature] Lt Cdr R.N. C.O. 800 Sqdn.		
				[signature] Lt Cdr R.N. C.O. No 13. C.A.G.		
July	3	Seafire 47	477	Self.	—	Strike on Kaishu Airfield, N.Kor.
"	3	"	460	"	"	C.A.P.
"	4	"	477	"	"	C.A.P.
"	17	"	477	"	"	Test Flight.
"	18	"	961	"	"	C.A.P.
"	18	"	489	"	"	C.A.P.

GRAND TOTAL [Cols. (1) to (10)] ....1676. Hrs.....45. Mins.

TOTALS CARRIED FORWARD

Right-hand page (flight times):

	SINGLE-ENGINE AIRCRAFT				MULTI-ENGINE AIRCRAFT						PASS. ENGER	INSTR/CLOUD FLYING [Incl. in cols. (1) to (10)]	
	DAY		NIGHT		DAY			NIGHT					
	Dual	Pilot	Dual	Pilot	Dual	1st Pilot	2nd Pilot	Dual	1st Pilot	2nd Pilot		Dual	Pilot
	(1)	(2)	(3)	(4)	(5)	(6)	(7)	(8)	(9)	(10)	(11)		
77	1440.25	1374.50	13.10	62.30	18.35	27.00	12.05	1.10	1.20	2.20	105.45	50.25	76.40
1		1.35											.15
1		1.30											
1		1.55											
1		1.55											.20
1		2.05											
1		1.35											
1		2.05											
7		12.40											.35 — 7 Deck Landings. 1 Catapult Launching.
		37.05											4.40 — 19 ... 4
													26/6/50 UNITED NATIONS IN ACTIVE SUPPORT OF SOUTH KOREANS AGAINST RUSSIAN SPONSORED NORTH KOREANS.
													TRIUMPH JOINED 7TH FLEET OFF KOREA
1		2.00											6 – 60lb R/P's fired at Hangars. Sampan Strafed!
		2.15											
1		2.05											.15
0		.10											
1		2.10											.30 — Recce of Utsuryo To Island.
	1460.25	1408.10	13.10	62.30	18.35	27.00	12.05	1.10	1.20	2.20	105.45	50.25	78.00
	(1)	(2)	(3)	(4)	(5)	(6)	(7)	(8)	(9)	(10)	(11)		(12)

Left:
Seafire 47s of 800 Squadron and Fireflys of 827 Squadron lined up on the deck of HMS *Triumph* as she leaves Malta for the Far East in August 1949. The disc on the muzzle of the cannon in the aircraft nearest the camera indicates that the guns were loaded.
FAA Museum

Above:
***Triumph's* Air Group disembarked at Sembawang, Singapore, early in 1950 before the outbreak of the war in Korea.**
FAA Museum

Right:
Shedding propeller blades, a Seafire 47 of 800 Squadron takes *Triumph's* barrier, off Singapore in January 1950. The pilot, Lt L. Stone, suffered burns when the plane caught fire immediately afterwards. The Seafire was a write-off. *FAA Museum*

take-offs or using RATOG we could launch at 15sec intervals (catapulting was a much slower business, with about one launch per minute). I did not use RATOG on that first mission, though I would on some of my later ones.

'During that first action nine Seafires of 800 Squadron and 12 Fireflys of 827 Squadron attacked Haeju airfield. We found no enemy planes there so we attacked on the hangars with rockets and cannon.'

At Haeju the attackers encountered little return fire. One Seafire was hit by a rifle-calibre round, another suffered minor damage to a radiator when it flew through debris thrown up by the explosions of its rocket projectiles when they hit the ground.

On the next day, 4 July, *Triumph* launched seven Seafires and 12 Fireflys to attack targets along the rail line between Yonan and Haeju. Following these initial strikes Task Force 77 withdrew from the combat zone. During the lull in operations

US and Royal Navy carrier planes in the war zone had black and white identification bands painted on their wings and fuselage, similar to those carried by Allied aircraft at the time of the Normandy invasion in 1944.

When the carrier air strikes resumed, on 18 July, it was agreed that *Triumph's* planes would provide combat air patrols (CAPs) and anti-submarine patrols to cover the Task Force, while the heavier and more effective US Navy attack planes struck at targets ashore. The results of the new policy were immediately evident: Handley's log book shows that he flew a CAP on 18 July, two on the 19th, then there was a break in the flying as Typhoon 'Grace' passed through the area and *Triumph* returned to Japan. Afterwards the carrier returned to the combat area and Handley flew two CAPs on the 25th, two on the 26th and two more on the 28th.

'Usually we carried a 50gal "torpedo" tank under the fuselage. In addition we could carry a 22½gal combat tank under each wing. The combat tanks were stressed for combat manoeuvres, but we did not like them because they reduced our maximum speed by about 20kt. They could be jettisoned, but as there were few spares we were ordered not to drop them except in a dire emergency. Shortage of range was never a problem for the Seafire 47s during the Korean conflict. All my flights were two hours or thereabouts and we always returned to the carrier with stacks of fuel.'

What of the wrinkling of the Seafire 47 rear fuselages, that would earlier have prevented these fighters from flying? As Tommy Handley explained, that problem was solved by ignoring it:

Left:
Seafires of 800 Squadron pictured shortly after landing at Iwakuni, Japan, in April 1950. Tommy Handley is on the left of the three pilots walking towards the camera. *Handley*

Right:
Wearing Korean War stripes and carrying two 22½gal underwing combat tanks, a Seafire 47 makes a low flypast over *Triumph* after a missed approach. *Handley*

Above:
HMS *Triumph* pictured at speed in the South China Sea in June 1950, with four Seafires and eight Fireflys ranged ready for launching. *Handley*

Right:
Seafire 47s ranged on the deck of *Triumph* prior to an air strike on North Korea. This picture was taken during one of the operations in July, before the black and white recognition bands were painted on the aircraft. *IWM*

'Soon after we began operations nearly all the Seafires had wrinkled rear fuselages. The wrinkling was not really visible to the human eye, but if you ran a hand over the skin you could detect the trouble spots. The worry was that the structure was less strong than it should have been. The Engineer Officer said they were outside the limits for peacetime flying — but he let them fly on operational sorties!

'We found that we had far fewer deck landing accidents once we started flying more. Flying on operations nearly every day, we became better at deck landings and aircraft were damaged less frequently.'

Throughout this period no enemy aircraft were encountered, and the CAP missions became routine. The only excitement occurred on 28 July, when a pair of Seafires intercepted a B-29 and Commissioned Pilot White moved in too close to the bomber. The latter's gunners either did not see or did not heed the recognition bands, and opened fire. The Seafire burst into flames and White baled out. Suffering from burns he was picked up from the sea by a US destroyer, and returned to *Triumph*.

Following this brief spell of operations, *Triumph* put into Kure dockyard for 10 days for maintenance. On 11 August the carrier went to sea again, this time to join the force mounting a blockade of the west coast of Korea, to prevent the enemy troops and supplies being carried south by sea. Again there were few targets to be found, however. On the 13th Handley took part in a rocket attack on oil storage tanks at Mokpo. On the 14th he flew a photo reconnaissance along the coast between Haishu and Chinnampo, his Seafire fitted with a single vertical camera; that afternoon he flew a CAP. On the 15th he flew a visual reconnaissance of the coast between Kunsan and Mokpo. On the 19th he flew a CAP. On the 20th he took part in an armed reconnaissance along the coast between Kunsan and Mokpo, during which he attacked a small naval craft with rockets and cannon. On the 21st he flew a reconnaissance mission and a CAP, did the same on the 26th and the same again on the 28th.

On 29 August Handley took part in another armed reconnaissance of the coast between Kunsan and Mokpo. This time the Seafires found two camouflaged motor junks and attacked them with rockets and cannon fire, leaving one on fire. Also on the 29th, 800 Squadron lost its commander, Lt-Cdr Ian MacLachlan, in a tragic accident on the carrier:

'Ian was in the Operations Room in the island, watching the aircraft landing through an open scuttle, when a Firefly went into the crash barrier. The wooden propeller blades broke off and a large piece from one of them flew through the scuttle and struck Ian on the head. He died a few hours later. It was a million-to-one-against accident.'

Following this loss, Tommy Handley was promoted to lieutenant-commander and assumed command of 800 Squadron.

By now the intensity of the operations was starting to tell on the Seafire force. On 1 September, 800 Squadron took delivery of the last of the replacement Seafire 47s

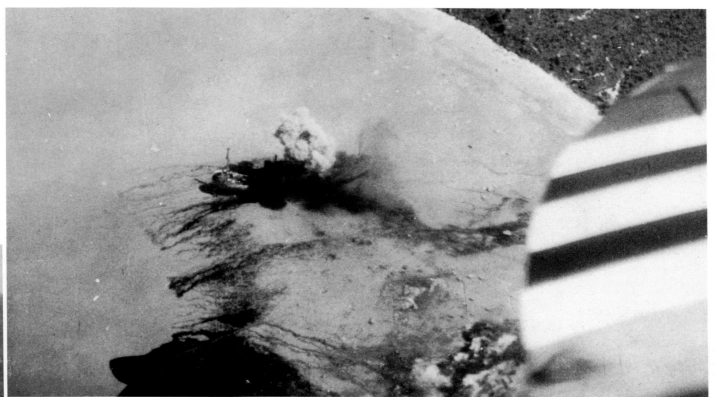

Above left:
Carrying a pair of 60lb rockets under each wing, a Seafire belches smoke from its RATOG as it gets airborne for a strike.
Handley

Left:
Fitted with rocket packs above the wing roots, a Seafire begins its take-off run. The bright ends of the rockets indicate that the rockets have just been fired but have not started to develop thrust. *IWM*

Above:
After a rocket attack on a North Korean vessel lying off Chinampo, a Seafire 47 took this oblique photo for damage assessment. *IWM*

held aboard the maintenance carrier HMS *Unicorn*. At the start of the conflict *Unicorn* had held 14 replacement Seafires, which had been issued to the carrier in order of quality starting with the best. The final replacements were the least satisfactory of those available, and in some cases were little better than the machines they replaced. A shortage of spare parts compounded the problems of the maintenance teams, and it was a rare day when 800 Squadron had more than eight Seafires available for operations. Nevertheless, by dint of much hard work, the unit usually put up a daily effort of around 25 sorties.

During September HMS *Triumph* took part in operations against rail targets along the west coast of Korea. On the 4th Handley led an armed reconnaissance of Kunsan, and on the 6th he flew a CAP over the cruiser HMS *Jamaica* while she bombarded the railway terminus there. On the 8th he escorted a Firefly attack on Wonsan, and afterwards the Seafires strafed patrol boats in the harbour. On the 10th bad weather halted air operations. He

flew a reconnaissance mission on the 15th and a CAP on the 17th. On 20 September Handley led an armed reconnaissance of the area around Chinnampo, which turned out to be the final operational mission by Seafires in Royal Navy service.

On 21 September HMS *Triumph* put in to Sasebo, Japan. The replacement carrier HMS *Theseus*, whose squadrons operated Sea Furys and Fireflys, was due to arrive in a few days. *Triumph* played no further part in the conflict and on 25 September she set sail for the United Kingdom. No 800 Squadron had started the conflict with 12 Seafires, and during its course the unit received 14 replacements for aircraft lost or damaged. The unit flew a total 360 operational sorties, of which 115 were against shipping or ground targets. The Seafires never encountered hostile aircraft and they suffered no losses from enemy action. But, non-combat attrition took a toll. As mentioned, one Seafire had been shot down in error by a 'friendly' B-29. Another was lost when its hook refused to lower, the pilot baled out and was picked up by a destroyer.

When *Triumph* left the operational area, 800 Squadron possessed nine flyable aircraft. But once the pressures of war had been removed, the unit's Engineer Officer re-asserted the peacetime rules and immediately declared six of the survivors unserviceable with wrinkled rear fuselages. At the end of 11 weeks of operations, of a total of 26 Seafires originally on strength or received as replacements, only three remained flyable.

With the departure of HMS *Triumph* from the Far East, the Seafire's career as a frontline fighter in the Royal Navy came to an end. 'We were,' as Tommy Handley put it, 'the last of the few . . .'

111

Above:
Spitfires and other types suffering 'the death of a thousand cuts' at an airfield in the Suez Canal Zone after the war.

Below:
Spitfire F24s broken up at Wroughton in Wiltshire before being sold as scrap.
Batchelor

War's End

You who have dared the holocaust:
You who have cleared the sky:
You who have held the shattered line:
You who have learned to die:
You who have swept the oceans:
You who have made cities burn:
You who have been death's right hand:
To what do you return?

It's hard tack and skilly, my lad,
And poverty for your lot;
A hero you were a week ago,
Now, nobody cares a jot.

R. P. L. Mogg